WATER UNDER
THE BRIDGE

WATER UNDER THE BRIDGE

WRITTEN AND PHOTOGRAPHED BY
JULIAN HOLLAND

COLLINS & BROWN

FRONT COVER

This ornate cast-iron bridge, built by the Britannia Foundry, Derby in 1837, marks the junction between the Oxford and Coventry Canals at Hawkesbury. To the right, the Oxford Canal passes through the Hawkesbury stop lock on its 77-mile journey to Oxford.

BACK COVER

Former lock keeper's cottage and stables at Old Ford Lock on the Regent's Canal in east London. The 200 acres of Victoria Park, London's oldest municipal park, forms the eastern boundary of the canal at this point. Just out of the picture to the left is the Royal Cricketers public house. Immediately to the south, the 1¼-mile Hertford Union Canal links the Regent's Canal with the River Lee Navigation.

First published in Great Britain in 1998
by Collins & Brown Ltd
London House
Great Eastern Wharf
Parkgate Road
London SW11 4NQ

All photographs © Julian Holland

Text © Collins & Brown Limited 1998

British Library Cataloguing in Publication Date:
A CIP catalogue record for this book is available from the British Library

ISBN 1-85585-688-3

Creative Director Julian Holland
Designed by Nigel White
Origination by Colour Symphony, Singapore
Printed in Hong Kong

Author's acknowledgements
I would like to thank the following individuals for their invaluable assistance in producing this book: David Titchener for processing the film; Francis Laver for loaning his camera when mine developed a fault; Nigel White for his hours spent on the computer and for the illustrations; last but not least to Sarah Laver for her map navigation, assistance at photographic locations and her continual support and encouragement.

HALF-TITLE PAGE

The attractively restored basin at Sowerby Bridge, Calder & Hebble Navigation.

TITLE PAGE

Two graceful cast-iron bridges, built by the Horseley Ironworks in the 1830s, span the triangular junction and island between the Oxford and Grand Union Canals at Braunston Turn.

CONTENTS

Calder &
Hebble
Navigation

Trent & Mersey
Canal

Shropshire
Union Canal

Worcester &
Birmingham
Canal

Oxford Canal

Stratford-upon-
Avon Canal

Regent's Canal

Gloucester &
Sharpness Canal

INTRODUCTION

Above *Broad Cut Top Lock on the outskirts of Wakefield, Calder & Hebble Navigation.*

*Seducing time along ribbons of winding water,
escaping the flurry, life's symphony of mania.
Drifting silently along, water under the bridge.*

THE CANAL AGE IN ENGLAND was short lived. However, its rapid growth brought about one of the greatest changes ever witnessed in this country – the Industrial Revolution. Until the mid-18th century, raw materials and goods had to be transported either by ship around the wreck-strewn coastline, by horse and cart on rutted and poorly maintained roads or on the treacherous, swirling currents of rivers. All these modes of transport were slow, inefficient and quite often dangerous.

The work of Thomas Newcomen and, later, James Watt in harnessing the power of steam during the 18th century provided the impetus for the rapid growth of the Industrial Revolution. The raw materials needed to ignite industry into action had to be transported to the gestating industrial and population centres of the Midlands and the North of England.

During the 17th century the navigation of some English rivers was improved by the building of locks to bypass dangerous weirs and, although these works brought some improvement to river transport, their benefits were only felt locally. The success of the Canal du Midi in France in the late 17th century was slow in filtering through to English engineers and industrialists. In fact, the very first canal with locks to be built in Britain was located in the north of Ireland – the Newry Canal was completed in 1742. This was followed by the St Helens Canal in Lancashire which was completed in 1757.

The first canal to be built that set the precedent for all those that followed was the Bridgewater Canal, engineered by James Brindley – the father of English canal builders. Coal had been mined on the Duke of Bridgewater's estate in Cheshire for many years but its transportation to the growing textile producing region around Manchester was inhibited by the slow and inefficient road system. The Duke commissioned Brindley to design and build the canal, thus linking his coal mines at Worsley to Manchester. It was completed in 1761 and was a resounding commercial success.

Stimulated by the major impact and prosperity of the Bridgewater Canal, there were soon many optimistic schemes being promoted to build a network of canals across the length and breadth of England. The period from 1761 to the early part of the 19th century saw an explosion of canal building, gradually forming a network of waterways that linked the industrial and population centres of the country. This period was before the introduction of earth-moving machines and the canals were carved through the English landscape by the blood, sweat and toil of thousands of unruly navvies. As the system expanded so did industry, and both shareholders and industrialists reaped their rewards. Ironically, for the working classes the subtopia of the industrial revolution had arrived.

Unfortunately, by the early 1830s the writing was on the wall for English canals. The development of the steam engine by Richard Trevithick and George Stephenson during the early 19th century had produced a vastly more efficient and faster form of transport. Railway Mania had arrived and its tracked tentacles soon touched every corner of the country. The newly opened railways were soon squeezing the life blood out of the canal companies. Many were taken over by railway companies only to be neglected and left to die a slow death. Unable to compete, the weed-choked waterways faced a bleak future but, fortunately for us now, the majority somehow managed to struggle through into the 20th century and on until World War II.

In 1948 many of the canals were nationalised by the Labour government, but this was all too late as commercial traffic on the system had ebbed away, not only to the railways but also to the short-sighted utopia of road transport. Commercial canal trade had virtually ceased to exist by the early 1960s. During this post-war period, people started

Above *The heavily locked section of the Oxford Canal at Napton, dominated by the restored windmill on the summit of 400ft-high Napton Hill.*

Left The Boat Museum at Ellesmere Port, the northern terminus of the Shropshire Union Canal, is Britain's premier canal museum. The museum is located in the historic and superbly restored dock complex situated on the waterfront overlooking the Manchester Ship Canal and the Mersey Estuary.

to discover the amenity value of these often hidden and tranquil waterways. Since then, to cater for an ever-increasing public interest, many of these canals have been improved, restored and currently there are many schemes in existence for the resuscitation of abandoned and derelict stretches of water.

The future has never looked better for the canals of England. As Thomas Telford, the doyen of canal engineers, once said, 'I admired commercial enterprise... but I hold that the aim and end of all ought not to be a mere bag of money, but something far higher and far better.' The endeavours of various individuals and groups involved in the resurrection of our canal heritage and legacy has allowed Telford's words to be realised.

In this book, I have set out to discover the history and portray the present day delights of a selected number of these English canals – all of them a living testimony to the optimistic dreams of their promoters, shareholders and builders. I hope you enjoy the journey!

Julian Holland Glastonbury, 1998

Left Residential canal boats and their well-tended gardens make a colourful sight at Little Venice. Overlooked by elegant houses in this peaceful part of London, the Regent's Canal starts its fascinating 8½-mile journey to Limehouse.

CALDER AND HEBBLE NAVIGATION

Above *Brightly painted narrowboats for hire await their next turn of duty at the well restored Sowerby Bridge Basin.*

THE RIVERS AIRE AND CALDER have been used by boats for hundreds of years. With the installation of locks and weirs in the late 17th and early 18th centuries, boats were able to reach Wakefield and Leeds from the Rivers Humber and Ouse thus greatly helping the development of the woollen and coal industries of the region. Further development of the waterway in the early 19th century led to a new inland port being built at Goole which gave the fast-growing industrial centres of Yorkshire direct access to the sea.

Once boats could reach Wakefield in 1700, there was pressure from the growing towns located further up the Calder Valley and the Hebble Valley for a waterway linking them to the outside world. By 1741 a survey of the proposed route had been carried out, involving making much of the Calder navigable as far as Halifax. However, this scheme was scuppered by landowners who were concerned about flooding and from owners of mills who felt that their water supplies would be diverted. Another 16 years elapsed before John Smeaton, engineer of the Eddystone Lighthouse, was asked to do a new survey on the route between Wakefield and Sowerby. He estimated the cost of building the navigation at £30,000 and a Bill was put before Parliament the following year. This time it was successful and Smeaton was appointed chief engineer for the project. Work started at Wakefield at the end of 1759 and within three years the lower part of the River Calder had been made navigable for boats. By the end of 1764 the navigation was open as far as Brighouse, where work stopped while money was raised to

Left A busy scene at the attractively located Salterhebble Locks. The summit of the navigation is at the top lock where the short Salterhebble Branch is all that remains of the heavily-locked branch to Halifax.

complete it to Sowerby Bridge. Smeaton was dismissed and James Brindley was appointed in his place to oversee the construction of the last section. Brooksmouth, the confluence of the Rivers Calder and Hebble, was reached by the beginning of 1766 and Salterhebble in the following year. By then, Brindley had departed to pastures new (the Rochdale Canal, the Staffordshire & Worcestershire and the Trent & Mersey) and he was replaced by Thomas Simpson. During late 1767 and early 1768 the newly opened section of the navigation was seriously damaged by a series of floods and the cost of repairs stretched the company's financial resources to the limit. By this date the company had spent nearly £65,000, as against Smeaton's estimate of £30,000, and Sowerby Bridge was still two miles to the west. The company was restructured, enabling it to borrow up to £20,000 to complete the navigation and, at the same time, tolls were raised on the section that was already in use. By mid-1769 the restructured company had

Right This many-arched railway viaduct carries the Bradford to Manchester trans-Pennine railway line across the navigation at Copley.

appointed Robert Carr as chief engineer, work restarted and the complete navigation to Sowerby Bridge was opened in September 1770.

To overcome the constant threat of flooding, floodgates were built to protect the man-made cuts that linked the navigable sections of the rivers. One of the benefits of the navigation was that coal from local mines now had an outlet to markets in Yorkshire. Coal was conveyed via a series of waggonways to wharves for transshipment and thence to the towns of Wakefield and Halifax. In 1776, the 3¾-mile Sir John Ramsden's Canal was opened, from Cooper Bridge on the Calder & Hebble, to Huddersfield, where it later linked with the Huddersfield Narrow Canal and thence to Manchester.

Over the next 20 years the Calder & Hebble flourished with the main traffic being locally mined coal, stone, wool, cloth and corn. Various improvements, including the construction of new cuts, rebuilding of locks and building of more warehouses, were carried out during this

Left *The rural setting of Broad Cut Top Lock. Beyond the railway bridge is the popular Navigation pub with gardens that reach down to the towpath. Opposite the pub are the remains of a staithe where coal was, until the early 1980s, loaded on to barges for transport to Thornhill Power Station.*

Above Although not a particularly attractive town, Brighouse does possess a pleasant basin which is located between the two locks.

period. Dividends to shareholders increased year-on-year, by 1794 reaching 13%. Then, in 1804, the 33-mile Rochdale Canal was opened, thus providing an important link over the Pennines between the Calder & Hebble at Sowerby Bridge and the Bridgewater Canal in Manchester. It was surveyed by John Rennie and engineered by William Jessop and its 92 locks were constructed to allow passage of a wide barge or two narrow boats. Extra wharves and warehouses were built at Sowerby Bridge to cope with the increase in traffic and the Calder & Hebble Company reduced their toll charges. With the opening of the Rochdale Canal, the Calder & Hebble became an important link in the series of waterways that stretched across Northern England from Hull to Manchester and business boomed.

To facilitate the transport of wool and cloth to and from Halifax, a short branch was opened from the main line at Salterhebble in 1828. The cost of building this 1¾-mile branch was nearly £60,000 – this being not far short of the original cost of the main line. The main reason for this was that over its short length the branch had no fewer than 14 locks and the installation of a pumping station to maintain water levels at the summit. To recoup this enormous cost the Calder & Hebble doubled the tolls charged for this short branch.

However, the opening of the Manchester & Leeds Railway in 1841 brought about a significant change in the Calder & Hebble's fortunes. The railway's route closely paralleled both the Calder & Hebble and the Rochdale Canal and soon both companies were having to reduce their tolls in face of the speedier competition. The railway also responded by cutting their charges and in March 1843 the Calder & Hebble was leased to the Manchester & Leeds Railway for a period of 14 years. This leasing arrangement was soon deemed illegal and the arrangement ended in 1847.

For the next eight years the Calder & Hebble was involved in various negotiations with the Aire & Calder with a view to the latter leasing the former. During this period tolls were reduced further but the navigation lost more of its traffic to the newly-opened railways. In 1855 the Aire & Calder agreed to lease the Calder & Hebble for a period of 21 years

– the neighbouring Rochdale Canal, upon which the Calder & Hebble depended for much of its through traffic, came under the control of several railway companies. The joint running of the Aire & Calder and Calder Hebble made much sense as considerable coal traffic still passed between the two waterways. A period of improvements followed, including extending some locks to the same length as those on the Rochdale Canal, but in 1885 the lease by the Aire & Calder ended and the improvements were never completed.

The Calder & Hebble passed into the early part of the 20th century with traffic slowly declining. World War I came and went and, despite strenuous efforts by the company to obtain more trade, matters did not improve – through traffic from the Rochdale Canal finally ended in 1937 and the Halifax branch was closed in 1942. Along with many other canals, the Calder & Hebble was nationalised in 1948 and the neighbouring Rochdale officially abandoned in 1952. Traffic to Sowerby Bridge completely ceased in 1955 and by the end of that decade the only commercial traffic being carried was coal for Thornhill power

Left *Cooper Bridge Lock where the navigation once again rejoins the River Aire. A short distance above the lock is the junction with the Huddersfield Broad Canal, opened in 1776 as Sir John Ramsden's Canal.*

Left *Some superb examples of modern grafitti adorn this former factory wall between Fall Ing Lock and Wakefield Flood Lock.*

station, near Dewsbury. Even this traffic ended in 1981 but in recent years the navigation has become increasingly popular as a cruising waterway for leisure craft.

A journey along the Calder & Hebble Navigation

Although the Calder & Hebble Navigation is only 21½ miles long, boat users have to negotiate a total of 33 locks, some of which are flood locks. Our journey starts at Fall Ing Lock in Wakefield, where the Aire & Calder Navigation forms an end-on junction with the Calder &

Left *A modern canal cruiser passes the British Waterways maintenance yard near Wakefield Flood Lock.*

Hebble. The city of Wakefield was once an important centre of cloth manufacturing and although this industry has now been eclipsed by cheap imports, there is still much evidence of its glorious past in the form of old mills and warehouses. Overlooking the city, the site of a famous 15th century battle in the Wars of the Roses, is the 250ft-high spire of the cathedral, its stonework blackened by centuries of industrial pollution.

The short, man-made cut from Fall Ing Lock ends at Wakefield Flood Lock, overlooked by the Jolly Sailor pub, where the navigation joins the course of the River Calder for the first time. On the southern outskirts of the city the navigation passes under a graceful, curving railway viaduct, its 95 brick arches providing a stark reminder of the onset of the Railway Age and the inevitable decline of the canals. Leaving the city behind, the navigation now takes a westerly course which it generally follows to its terminus at Sowerby Bridge. At Thornes Lock the navigation leaves the course of the river and passes through a short man-made cut, protected at its westerly end by Thornes Flood Lock, one of many that were built to protect the man-made cuts from river flood water. A unique feature of the Calder & Hebble is that most of the locks gates are operated with a unique handspike instead of a windlass.

For the next mile the navigation joins the course of the river, passing under the M1 motorway before entering Broad Cut at the Broad Cut Low Lock. Between here and the Top Lock is the attractive and popular Navigation public house, conveniently located for towpath walkers and boat users in the shadow of a railway viaduct. Less than 20 years ago, coal was still being conveyed by barge from wharves near here to Thornhill Power Station, close to Dewsbury. Broad Cut leads on to Horbury Cut, the beginning of a five-mile section of man-made cuts that closely parallel the river as far as Thornhill Flood Lock. At Horbury Bridge, where the Bingley Arms and the Ship are two canalside pubs, a disused lock marks a former connection with the river. The navigation follows a straight course for over a mile to the two Figure of Three Locks and the site of another disused lock down to the river.

Mill Bank Lock and the following Long Cut leads to the junction with the short Dewsbury Arm. Until 1790, when the Thornhill Cut was opened, this was the route of the original main line. The arm ends at Savile Town Basin where there is now a boat hire company, boatyard, moorings and museum. Returning to the main line, the Calder & Hebble passes through Thornhill Double Locks to Brewery Bridge, where the Nelson public house is conveniently situated overlooking the canal, and continues under railway bridges to Thornhill Flood Lock. Here, the navigation joins company with the river for a short distance to Greenwood Lock.

Leaving behind the industrial outskirts of Dewsbury, the navigation passes through Greenwood Flood Gates and Shepley Bridge Lock, where several more pubs provide an opportunity for refreshment, soon entering a steep-sided and wooded valley as far as Mirfield. This is an attractive canalside location with boatyard and pub on the southern outskirts of the town. Nearby, Mirfield railway station is also extremely handy for towpath walkers wishing to return to Wakefield. Immediately to the west, the navigation encounters Ledgard Bridge Flood Lock and Battyeford Lock, where the Pear Tree Inn is located in a picturesque setting overlooking the River Calder. Passing under the railway line, the navigation follows a meandering course through Battye Flood Gates, Cooper Bridge Lock and Cooper Bridge Flood Gates.

Cooper Bridge is the junction with the Huddersfield Broad Canal. This 3¼-mile canal, originally known as Sir John Ramsden's Canal, was opened to Huddersfield in 1776. When the Huddersfield Narrow Canal opened in 1811 it formed part of a cross-Pennine route to Manchester. In 1945, the Huddersfield Broad Canal (then owned by the London Midland & Scottish Railway) was sold to the Calder & Hebble Navigation for £4000. At the same time the Huddersfield Narrow Canal was abandoned, thus severing the link with Manchester. Opposite Cooper Bridge Junction are the grounds of 16th century Kirklees Hall where Robin Hood is reputed to have been buried. Proceeding on its meandering course up the wooded valley, the Calder & Hebble soon encounters the two Kirklees Locks, passing under the M62 motorway close to Anchor Pit Lock. Ahead is Brighouse, a former woollen

Above *This view of Salterhebble middle lock clearly shows the generous dimensions of the Calder & Hebble Navigation which enabled wide-beam barges to travel up to Sowerby Bridge and then on to the Rochdale Canal.*

producing town that provided an important source of traffic for the Calder & Hebble in the late 18th and early 19th centuries. The route of the canal through the town has been attractively landscaped and Brighouse Basin provides moorings and a boatyard. Several pubs in the town, including the New Tavern, the Anchor Inn and the Prince of Wales, are conveniently located close to the canal.

Beyond Brighouse, the Calder & Hebble burrows into the valley of the River Calder with the hills pressing in ever closer on both sides. The canal, river and railway keep close company for the last six miles to Sowerby Bridge. Set in wooded surroundings, Ganny Lock, Brookfoot Lock, Cromwell Lock and Park Nook Lock pass in quick succession. Passing the conveniently located Colliers Arms, the Calder & Hebble negotiates Elland Lock and passes under a railway bridge before emerging at the picturesque Elland Basin. Grouped around the basin are restored warehouses and the Barge & Barrel public house, while close to Elland Bridge are two more pubs.

Leaving Elland behind, the Calder & Hebble rounds a bend in the valley before climbing up through Woodside Mills Lock and Long Lee Lock to the three attractively located Salterhebble Locks. At the top lock, the summit of the canal, is the junction with the short Salterhebble Branch. This is all that remains of the short, heavily-locked branch to Halifax that was opened in 1828 and abandoned in 1942. The town of Halifax, once a centre of the woollen industry, lies to the north but is well worth a detour to visit the museums that bring to life its glorious, industrial heritage.

From Salterhebble, a two-mile long summit pound takes the Calder & Hebble along the side of the Hebble Valley to its terminus at Sowerby Bridge. The restored warehouses around the basin form a fitting tribute to the optimism of the 18th century canal builders. Here, there are boatyards, boat hire companies, moorings and several canalside pubs. Dominated by the town, with its old mill chimneys, the Calder & Hebble ends at Albert Wood Lock. Beyond this point, the heavily-locked Rochdale Canal once commenced its tortuous journey across the Pennines to Manchester.

The Rochdale Canal was one of three trans-Pennine canals, the other two being the Leeds & Liverpool and the Huddersfield Narrow Canal, and was surveyed by John Rennie and engineered by William Jessop. It opened in 1804 and formed an important 33-mile link between the Bridgewater Canal in Manchester and the Calder & Hebble at Sowerby Bridge. Its 92 wide locks were constructed to allow passage of a barge or two narrow boats and until the mid-19th century was commercially successful. However, as with its two rivals, decline set in due to competition from the railways and the last commercial boat passed along its length in 1937. Although not nationalised in 1948 it was officially abandoned in 1952. With the revival of the Ashton and Peak Forest Canals during the 1970s the short section within Manchester was restored to provide a link in the Cheshire Ring. The remainder, which passes through dramatic Pennine scenery and which provides for a spectacular towpath walk, is now the subject of full scale restoration. Perhaps, in the not too distant future, boats will once again be able to travel from Wakefield to Manchester via the Calder & Hebble Navigation and the Rochdale Canal.

Left The attractively restored warehouses and basin at Sowerby Bridge. On the hill in the distance is the 250ft Wainhouse Tower, built in the late 19th century and now a prominent landmark in the district.

GLOUCESTER & SHARPNESS CANAL

FROM MEDIEVAL TIMES the River Severn, England's longest river, was an important trade route linking the port of Bristol with the Midlands. Boats could travel as far north as Bewdley and Welshpool but, due to the strong tidal nature of the river with its shifting sand banks and shoals, the passage of commercial traffic became increasingly difficult and dangerous. A cargo-carrying shallow draught sailing ship, known as the Severn trow, was developed to assist passage along this notorious waterway and, until the 19th century, barges were still being hauled up the river by gangs of men. In the late 16th century the city of Gloucester received a royal charter giving it formal status as a port and a custom house was built. Inevitably, as the ships became larger and heavier, so the navigational problems increased. With the dawn of the Industrial Revolution the river became even more vital, linking as it did the coalfields and growing industries of the Midlands with the Bristol Channel and the coastal ports of Britain.

By the late 18th century serious proposals had been put forward to build a canal linking Gloucester and Berkeley Pill, thus bypassing the most dangerous part of the river. However, a canal linking the Rivers Severn and Thames was the first on the scene. This was in fact two separate undertakings, the Stroudwater Canal and the Thames & Severn Canal. Opened in 1779 the 8-mile Stroudwater Canal was built to link the wool-producing town of Stroud with the navigable River Severn at Framilode. The Thames & Severn Canal was opened in 1789 from Stroud to the River Thames at Lechlade and abandoned in 1933. Commercial traffic continued on the Stroudwater until 1941 before it was officially abandoned in 1954.

Following the opening of the Stroudwater Canal the businessmen of

Above *Victoria Basin in Gloucester Docks houses some of the floating exhibits of the National Waterways Museums. The museum is housed on three floors of the elegant red brick Llanthony Warehouse and tells the story of Britain's inland waterways.*

Gloucester were soon clamouring to improve the port status of their city. The Gloucester Canal Committee was formed and in 1792 they asked Robert Mylne to obtain an Act of Parliament for the new Gloucester & Berkeley Canal. With much foresight the canal was designed to enable sea-going vessels of up to 300 tons to reach the city of Gloucester. There was no restriction on the height of vessels as all the bridges were to be of the lifting type. In short, it was to be the widest and deepest ship canal in the world. With an estimated cost of £137,000 for construction of the canal, the Act was passed on 25 March 1793 and by September of that year Mylne had been appointed as Chief Engineer. Work on the Gloucester canal basin commenced in 1794 but appalling weather conditions soon brought this to a halt. From the beginning, the Canal Committee members were continually bickering among themselves and with the Chief Engineer. Progress was slow and problems were soon encountered with the original contractors so, in 1795, the inexperienced

Left Patch Bridge is conveniently situated close to the Tudor Arms public house and half a mile south-east of the world-famous Slimbridge Wildfowl & Wetlands Trust.

Left *Splatt Bridge, near Frampton-on-Severn's 14th-century Church of St Mary, and one of the attractive Classical-style lock-keeper's cottages that are unique to the Gloucester & Sharpness Canal.*

James Dadford was appointed as Resident Engineer. During that year the excavation of the Gloucester basin and the first stretch of the canal to Hempsted seemed to be progressing well. However, it soon became apparent that the original estimate of the cost for constructing the canal was wildly inaccurate. Additional funding had to be found and in May 1797 a further Act of Parliament was obtained to raise permitted capital to £200,000. In 1798 Mylne was dismissed as Chief Engineer and James Dadford assumed authority. By 1799 only the lock from the River Severn, the Gloucester basin and five and half miles of canal had been built and of the £200,000 raised only £15,000 had actually been spent on construction. Where the rest of the money went has been open to speculation ever since. Charles Dadford was also dismissed and the whole project came to a grinding halt.

For the next sixteen years the unfinished canal lay dormant, Robert Mylne having died in 1811. This was during the period of the Napoleonic War and at its end in 1815 the demobbed soldiers and sailors formed a large and untapped workforce. To help overcome the spectre of mass unemployment, the Government of the day set up a commission with the authority to issue loans to schemes that involved work for unskilled labour. The near-bankrupt Gloucester & Berkeley Canal Company jumped at this opportunity and lost no time in applying to the Commission for a loan of £125,000 – the amount estimated to complete construction. At the same time the proposed southern end of the canal was changed from Berkeley Pill to Sharpness.

Thomas Telford, the celebrated canal engineer, had been appointed by the Government commission to oversee the company's loan application and his subsequent report was favourable. Work restarted and in 1820 a junction had been formed with the Stroudwater Canal at Saul but soon further problems were encountered with increasing costs and a rapid turnover of resident engineers. By the end of 1821 the Government Commission had lost patience and took over the uncompleted canal. Construction stopped again and was not restarted until the autumn of 1822 when the canal company appointed yet another contractor and obtained a further loan. Eventually the 15¾-mile

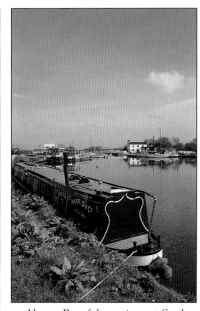

Above *Peaceful moorings at Saul Junction, once a busy junction with the Stroudwater Canal. The latter canal, together with the Thames & Severn Canal, is now the subject of a restoration scheme by the Cotswold Canals Trust which eventually plans to once again link England's two major rivers.*

canal was completed, 34 years after the passing of the Act of Parliament, and officially opened amidst much ceremony on 26 April 1827. Commercial trade on the canal was soon flourishing and Gloucester became a thriving inland port. In later years, improvements to the River Severn between Gloucester and Worcester, the enlargement of Sharpness Docks and the purchase of the Worcester & Birmingham Canal by the Sharpness New Docks Company in 1874 further enhanced Gloucester's prime position. Commercial traffic, mainly timber, grain and oil, continued well into the 1960s and although this trade has disappeared the Gloucester & Sharpness Canal is now a popular waterway for leisure cruising.

A journey along the Gloucester & Sharpness Canal
Until the opening of the Severn Bridge in the 1960s, the historic city of Gloucester was strategically located at the lowest bridge crossing of the

Right The main basin at Gloucester Docks is surrounded by elegant red brick Victorian warehouses, many of which have been superbly restored and converted into offices, restaurants, bars, museums and antique markets. After the magnificent cathedral, Gloucester Docks is now the city's major tourist attraction.

River Severn. For centuries the city had been the gateway to South Wales and as such became an important Roman garrison town and medieval city. Gloucester Cathedral, one of the finest medieval buildings in Britain with its magnificent stained glass windows and the tomb of King Edward II, is within a short distance of Gloucester Docks. This is the northern terminus of the Gloucester & Sharpness Canal and the start of our journey down the canal.

The dock basin at Gloucester became fully operational in 1827 when the canal was eventually completed. Soon the docks were busy with Severn trows, canal narrow boats and sea-going sailing ships. Corn, timber and wine were among the major imports while the main export was salt which was conveyed down the Severn from Worcester. An extra basin, corn warehouses, timber yards and quays soon had to be built to cope with the increased trade. Both the Midland Railway and Great Western Railway were linked to the docks by a network of railway lines that threaded the quays and surrounding streets. The enlargement of Sharpness Docks in 1874 brought about a reduction in sea-going vessels arriving in Gloucester. Instead, goods were transshipped on to barges and, if bound for the Midlands, passed through Gloucester without unloading and this, in turn, brought about a decline in the use of the warehouses at Gloucester. Commercial traffic subsequently increased in the 1920s when barges carrying petroleum from Avonmouth regularly passed through Gloucester Docks en route to Worcestershire. This continued well into the 1960s but, with the growing competition from road transport, commercial traffic from Sharpness to Gloucester had virtually ceased by 1980.

Today, Gloucester Docks has taken on a new role as a major tourist and leisure attraction. Access from the River Severn into the canal basin is provided by Gloucester Lock, located at the northern end of the main basin and first used in 1812. The basin is still surrounded by the elegant red brick Victorian warehouses which have been sympathetically converted to offices, restaurants, shops and museums. In recent years the backdrop of the warehouses and docks has provided excellent location material for several major television dramas, including the BBC

Above *The sailing ship* Midsummer *undergoing repairs in the dry dock at Gloucester.*

Above *A restored railway crane on the quayside at Gloucester Docks. Beyond, the Lock Warehouse, now a large antiques centre, overlooks Gloucester Lock and the canal's northerly link with the River Severn.*

TV series 'The Onedin Line'. Pleasure craft, converted narrow boats and the occasional sail-training vessel line the quays of both the main basin and Victoria Basin. The National Waterways Museum and British Waterways Archive Office are housed in a beautifully converted warehouse overlooking the Barge Arm off the main basin.

The National Waterways Museum opened in 1988 and is housed on three floors of Llanthony Warehouse within which is told the 200-year story of inland waterways via working models, archive film, interactives and hands-on exhibits. Outside, around two sides of the quay, are boats of all shapes and sizes and old railway wagons and wagon turntables. Boat trips are operated from the museum aboard 'Queen Boadicea II', built in 1936 as a Thames passenger ship and used at the evacuation of Dunkirk in 1940. Between April and October daily 45 minute duration trips operate on the Gloucester & Sharpness Canal with longer day cruises to Sharpness or Tewkesbury. In the summer months longer evening cruises are also available up the River Severn. (The National Waterways Museum, Llanthony Warehouse, Gloucester Docks, Gloucester GL1 2EH. Tel. 01452 318054. Open daily except Christmas Day.) The Robert Opie Collection, a museum of advertising and packaging, is housed in the nearby Albert Warehouse. (Robert Opie Collection, Albert Warehouse, Gloucester Docks, Gloucester. Tel. 01452 302309. Open daily except Mondays.)

Boats proceeding to Sharpness have to pass under the modern electrically-operated Llanthony bascule bridge which guards the southern end of the main basin. South of the bridge the elegant Pillar Warehouse on Bakers Quay has now become a popular canalside pub and restaurant. For some distance the canal is flanked by old warehouses, maltings, timber yards and flour mills. The former Gloucester Railway Carriage & Wagon Works which once backed on to the east bank of the canal has long since disappeared and been replaced by a modern retail and leisure park. To the west of the canal are the remains of Llanthony Priory, founded by Augustinian monks in the 12th century. The canal is then bordered by unattractive modern industrial units and more timber yards until Hempsted Bridge and the

Right *Elegant Victorian warehouses are mirrored in the still waters of the dock basin at Gloucester.*

Above *Sellars Bridge and the Pilot Inn overlook a steep-sided cutting close to a former oil wharf that saw some of the last commercial trade on the Gloucester & Sharpness Canal.*

beginning of the towpath to Sharpness is reached. This is the first of fifteen traditional manually-operated wooden swing-bridges that cross the canal between here and Sharpness. The village of Hempsted, now part of Gloucester's spreading suburbs, contains the 14th-century church of St Swithun, 17th-century Hempsted House and a medieval village cross.

Now out into open country, the canal soon executes a sharp S-bend just before Simms and Rea Bridges are reached. The latter bridge is guarded by the first of the single-storey classical-style bridge-keeper's cottages whose style is unique to this canal. The village of Stonebench, one of the best locations to view the mighty Severn Bore, is but a short distance to the west. The river has one of the highest tidal variations in the world, sometimes reaching a height of up to 40ft during spring tides. For a short distance the canal passes close to a meandering bend of the River Severn before swinging back inland to pass a former oil wharf that was once supplied by barge from Avonmouth. Sellars Bridge and the popular Pilot public house are but a short distance further on. A patchwork of apple and pear orchards in this flat farmland of the Severn Vale are testimony to the cider and perry-drinking activities of the Severn boatmen. Teams of men once towed boats up river and their thirst was quenched at the many long-vanished riverside drinking houses that once lined this meandering waterway.

Continuing south, the Gloucester & Sharpness Canal passes under Hardwicke Bridge, closely bordering the nearby grounds of Hardwicke Court to the east. The canal now follows a fairly straight route for one -and-a-half miles through a pastoral setting to Parkend Bridge where there are boat moorings. The peaceful village of Epney and the riverside Anchor Inn is but a short detour westwards from the bridge. Between Parkend Bridge and Saul Junction, a further one-and-a-half miles to the south, the canal is carried above the surrounding farmland on a low embankment.

Saul Junction, approached through yet another lift bridge and now a peaceful mooring with a boatyard, was once an important junction with the Stroudwater Canal. Opened in 1779 the 8-mile canal was built to link the wool-producing town of Stroud with the navigable River Severn at Upper Framilode. Commercial traffic consisted of locally produced wool and coal from the Forest of Dean. Ten years later the ill-fated Thames & Severn Canal was opened from Stroud to the River Thames at Lechlade, but this important connection never fulfilled its promotors' dreams due to faulty engineering work and the difficulties encountered when navigating the Upper Thames. However trade on the Stroudwater improved when the Gloucester & Sharpness Canal was opened to Saul Junction in 1820. Following the abandonment of the Thames & Severn in 1933 commercial traffic continued on the Stroudwater until 1941 before being officially abandoned in 1954. The Stroudwater Canal Society was founded in 1972, eventually becoming the Stroudwater, Thames & Severn Canal Trust. Since then the Trust has done much work in restoring sections of both canals although much remains to be done before the canal can once again carry traffic (for details of the Trust's aims and work contact Cotswold Canals Trust Offices, The Flat Offices, Cotswold District Council Depot, Chesterton Lane, Cirencester, Gloucestershire GL7 1YE. Tel. 01285 643440). The Thames & Severn Way long distance path follows the canal westwards from Saul Junction to Upper Framilode and eastwards to Stroud and Lechlade. A short section of the canal is still in water at Saul where it is used for moorings.

From Saul Junction the Gloucester & Sharpness Canal continues in a south-westerly direction, passing Sandfield Bridge and a former canal-linked Cadbury's chocolate factory, to Fretherne Bridge where the Severn Way long distance path joins the towpath for the remainder of its route to Sharpness. At this point a short detour on foot to the nearby picturesque village of Frampton-on-Severn is highly recommended. The village is famed for its 22-acre village green, the largest in England, which contains a cricket pitch and three ponds. The wide green is flanked by Georgian and half-timbered houses and the 18th-century Frampton Court. The Bell Hotel and the Three Horseshoes are both popular public houses also overlooking the green. Located at the southern end of the village, close to the east bank of the canal and

Above *The disused lock gate of the Stroudwater Canal at Saul Junction. Junction Bridge House stands guard over the swing bridge and the junction with a restored section of the Stroudwater.*

Above A peaceful scene at Fretherne Bridge, between Frampton-on-Severn and Saul, overlooked by another of the attractive Classical-style lock keeper's cottages. Just beyond the bridge the former Cadbury's chocolate factory was once the destination of much canal-borne trade from the Midlands.

Splatt Bridge, is the pretty 14th-century Church of St Mary.

Retracing our steps to Fretherne Bridge the canal follows a more-or-less dead straight southerly line for two miles to Cam Bridge. En route the canal passes Frampton-on-Severn church and another of the attractive and diminutive Doric bridgekeeper's houses at Splatt Bridge, a popular location for anglers. Just before Cam Bridge a small feeder arm joins the canal with water that has flowed down from the Cotswold escarpment. A further mile through the low-lying pastoral landscape lies Shepherd's Patch and Patch Bridge, the thirteenth of the lifting bridges on the canal. The small settlement of Shepherd's Patch contains a youth hostel, the popular canalside Tudor Arms public house and a caravan park. The Slimbridge Wildfowl & Wetlands Trust is located just half a mile to the west of Patch Bridge. The Trust was founded by the late Sir Peter Scott in 1946 as a sanctuary for wildfowl and, with 150 different species, has become the largest collection of its kind in the world. During the winter months the 1000 acres of water meadows, set on the east bank of the River Severn, are home to literally thousands of migrating birds. The public has access to waymarked paths and hides, a visitor centre, restaurant and shops. The Trust, world-famous for its research work and for its role in saving many species from extinction, is open to the public each day (Tel. 01453 890333).

From Patch Bridge, the Gloucester & Sharpness Canal wends its way across peaceful, flat farmland with the floodbank of the Severn Estuary but a short distance to the north west. After two miles the twin lifting bridges at the small village of Purton are reached. The canal executes a last, sweeping bend to run alongside the flood bank of the Severn, passing a large water treatment works and former timber ponds. Just before its entry to Sharpness Docks the canal passes the site of the Severn Railway Bridge. Spanning both the canal and the river the 22-span Severn Railway Bridge, opened in 1879, was, until the opening of the Severn Tunnel in 1886, the shortest railway route between Bristol and South Wales. Unfortunately, this graceful cast-iron structure was badly damaged in November 1959 when two oil tankers collided in thick fog with the bridge and brought down the central spans. The bridge was eventually demolished and only the remains of a few stone piers and the base of the one moveable span across the canal can still be seen.

Once bustling with sea-going ships, canal boats and barges, the quays and warehouses of Sharpness Docks are much quieter now that commercial traffic to Gloucester and beyond has disappeared. The old dock basin, once connected to the River Severn by a now-disused lock, provides moorings for pleasure craft. Serious problems were encountered during the construction of this basin when, in 1825, a dam built at Sharpness to protect the dock from the River Severn was demolished by a 33ft-high tide. The few sea-going ships that do visit Sharpness enter the docks via a lock from the River Severn that is only accessible during high tides. Despite this lack of commercial traffic the Gloucester & Sharpness Canal has, in recent years, seen an upturn in its fortunes with the waterway being used by an increasing number of pleasure craft as an important link with the canals of the Midlands.

Right The tranquil setting of the original basin and Old Dock House of the Gloucester & Sharpness Canal at Sharpness. Directly beyond the protecting stone wall lies the half-mile wide estuary of the River Severn.

Above This massive stone edifice, sandwiched between the river and canal a short distance north-east of Sharpness Docks, is all that remains of the 22-span Severn Railway Bridge. Until the bridge was demolished following collision damage in 1959 this stone structure supported a swing bridge that spanned the canal, allowing the passage of high masted ships.

SHROPSHIRE UNION CANAL

Above *To the south of Brewood the attractively balustraded Avenue Bridge carries the tree-lined private drive to nearby Chillington Hall.*

THE SHROPSHIRE UNION CANAL, linking the estuary of the River Mersey with the West Midlands, was formed by the amalgamation of three separate canal companies. The first of these to be built was the Chester Canal which was originally planned to tap into the lucrative trade to and from the Potteries by linking the River Dee at Chester with the Trent & Mersey Canal at Middlewich. An Act of Parliament to enable the canal to be built for wide beam boats was passed in 1772. Construction work started at Chester in the same year but progress was slow due to engineering problems, financial difficulties and disputes with the separate River Dee Company over the river lock at Chester. Due to pressure from the Trent & Mersey Canal, who saw this new canal as a threat to their trade, the planned route of the Chester Canal was altered so that it terminated at Nantwich instead of Middlewich. However, the Chester Canal Company's optimism about large salt deposits being found in the Nantwich area soon came to nought when this trade never materialised. Middlewich and the junction with the Trent & Mersey was not reached until 1833 when a 10-mile branch was built from Barbridge Junction. From the start, the Chester Canal was doomed to failure on its own and by the end of 1787 the company had no cash left for urgently needed repairs to Beeston lock. All commercial traffic south of this point ceased until 1790 when new-found optimism over proposed links with the planned Ellesmere Canal enabled the canal to reopen.

The second of the canals that eventually formed the Shropshire Union was the Ellesmere Canal. This was an ambitious plan to link the River Mersey with the River Severn, via the River Dee and Ellesmere. Engineered by William Jessop, the first part of this scheme, an 8¾-mile

Left *Located close to the lower end of the Audlem flight of 15 locks are the tranquil moorings at picturesque Audlem Wharf. The restored building of Audlem Mill is now a convenient canal shop and workshop and nearby are the Bridge and Shroppie Fly canalside pubs.*

Above A cast-iron milepost set in the leafy cutting south of Brewood gives the distances to Autherley Junction, Norbury Junction and Nantwich.

wide beam canal between Ellesmere Port on the River Mersey and Chester, was opened in 1795. Two years later, the link was made with the Chester Canal in the city and hence opened up a route via the locked Dee Branch down to the River Dee. However, the planned connection from here to the Shrewsbury, via Ruabon and Ellesmere was never fully completed. Although sections and various branches were built they were not connected to the outside world until a branch was opened in 1805 from Hurleston Junction on the Chester Canal. Included in this once land-locked system is Thomas Telford's massive Pontcyscyllte Aqueduct, still one of the wonders of the British canal system. The section from Hurleston Junction to Llantisilio, via Ellesmere, Chirk, Pontcysyllte and Llangollen is now known as the Llangollen Canal.

The opening of the northern section of the Ellesmere Canal and the connection at Hurleston brought increased trade to the impoverished Chester Canal and by 1813 the two companies amalgamated to become the Ellesmere & Chester Canal. However, this newly formed company still did not have any links with the flourishing industrial area of the Midlands. This all changed in 1825 when an Act of Parliament was passed enabling the building of the Birmingham & Liverpool Junction Canal between Nantwich, then the southern terminus of the Ellesmere & Chester Canal, and Autherley Junction with its links to the Birmingham Canal Network via the Staffordshire & Worcestershire Canal.

The Birmingham & Liverpool Junction was the missing link in the trio of canals that were to eventually amalgamate to form the Shropshire Union. The Act of Parliament enabling the building of this canal and authorising the raising of up to £½ million was passed in May 1826. Thomas Telford was appointed chief engineer and by the autumn of that year the whole route had been surveyed. In contrast to the Ellesmere & Chester Canal's wide beam route from Nantwich to Ellesmere Port, the locks on the new canal were designed for narrow boats. The latest cut-and-fill construction techniques were to be used, thus enabling the route to be more direct without reverting to contour-

Right Narrowboat Laurel approaches Bridge 55 at Goldstone Wharf. Just beyond the bridge is a canalside pub, the Wharf Tavern, that is located in a former warehouse.

hugging. Work commenced at Nantwich in early 1827 but major problems were soon encountered with heavy rain and landslips during the construction of embankments and cuttings. By 1832, with progress being continually interrupted by major slippages, the canal company had run out of money. To add further to the company's woes, the health of Thomas Telford was also deteriorating. The company was forced to borrow money so that work could continue and by the end of the year the canal was open between Nantwich and Norbury.

To the south of Norbury was the major stumbling block to the canal's southward progress. Using the cut-and-fill technique, the giant embankment at Shorbury was built with millions of tons of spoil excavated from Grub Street cutting, 1½-miles to the north. Thousands of navvies toiled over its construction for more than five years, constantly being interrupted by slippages and seriously delaying the opening of the whole canal. By 1834 the rest of the canal was complete but still the embankment remained unfinished. Telford died in

Right A magnificently restored example of one of Thomas Clayton's fleet of commercial narrowboats awaits passage through the Adderley flight of locks.

September of that year, to be replaced as chief engineer by the young William Cubitt. By July of 1835 the embankment and thus the canal was eventually completed, but the long drawn-out and disastrous construction period had considerably added to the company's financial problems. The final cost of £800,000 was double the original estimate and shareholders did not even receive one penny for their investment. Apart from the Manchester Ship Canal, the Birmingham & Liverpool Junction was the last major canal to be built in Britain – just as the dawn of the Railway Age was breaking.

One fly in the ointment was the Staffordshire & Worcestershire Canal Company's plan to extort large tolls on boats travelling the half mile from Autherley Junction, at the southern end of the B&LJ to Aldersley Junction, the western end of the Birmingham Canal. To thwart the Staffs & Worcs, the B&LJ drew up plans for the Tettenhall & Autherley Canal which would have crossed over the Staffs & Worcs on an aqueduct. Just the threat of this was enough to make the Staffs & Worcs reduce their tolls by 85%.

While the sad saga of the Birmingham & Liverpool Junction Canal was unfolding, the neighbouring Ellesmere & Chester Canal started construction of the 10-mile branch from their main line at Barbridge Junction to a junction with the Trent & Mersey at Middlewich. This canal with four narrow beam locks was completed in 1833, over half a century after it was originally proposed, providing the long sought-after link with the The Potteries.

The complete system was now in place but it was all too late, for the Railway Age was just dawning. In the face of this looming competition, the Ellesmere & Chester greatly enlarged facilities at Ellesmere Port in 1840 and the Birmingham & Liverpool Junction introduced passenger fly boat services in 1843. The two companies worked closely together and in 1845 the B&LJ was absorbed into the Ellesmere & Chester, thus creating a major network of canals that linked the West Midlands, The Potteries, Shropshire, Wales and the River Mersey. In the following year, this newly formed company was renamed the Shropshire Union Railways & Canal Company. Behind this change of name was a plan to

Above *The cut-and-fill method of construction used by Thomas Telford for building the Birmingham & Liverpool Junction Canal is evident in this photograph of the steep-sided Woodseave Cutting.*

Above *Looking north under Bridge 42 near High Offley. Nearby is the isolated Anchor Inn where boat users and towpath walkers can enjoy a quiet pint in the canalside garden.*

build new railway lines and to convert the canals into railways. The only railway that was actually built by this new company was the line linking Stafford with Shrewsbury, opened in 1849, but the latter conversion option was never exercised.

In 1847 the London & North Western Railway leased the Shropshire Union Railways & Canal Company and, unlike other railway takeovers of canals, developed a positive attitude towards development of trade on the system. No doubt this was partly due to the Shropshire Union's branches penetrating into the territory of the L&NWR's competitor, the Great Western Railway. Despite competition from the railways, most of the canal system flourished and remained profitable until the early 20th century. Under the expert guidance of the new Chief Engineer, George Jebb, the Shropshire Union system was gradually improved and, to cope with ever-increasing trade, its fleet of narrowboats had increased to 450 by the turn of the century.

Prior to World War I the L&NWR had subsidised some of the loss-making branches of the Shropshire Union. From 1914 to 1918 these subsidies were paid by the Government and it was the withdrawal of them at the end of the war that started the gradual decline from which the canal company was never to recover. The previously paternalistic L&NWR refused to reintroduce the subsidies and in 1921 the canal company was forced to sell off its fleet of narrowboats. In the ensuing financial climate, maintenance standards inevitably deteriorated and locks were closed to traffic at weekends. The Shropshire Union network was purchased outright by the L&NWR in 1922 and, in turn, this railway (and thus the canal) became part of the larger London Midland & Scottish Railway in the Railway Grouping of 1923. The decline continued and by 1944 the Shropshire Union system, apart from the main line between Autherley Junction and Ellesmere Port and the short Middlewich branch, was officially closed. However, the Llangollen Canal did survive as it was an important source of water supply from the River Dee and has now become one of the most popular cruising waterways in the country.

As with many other canals the Shropshire Union was nationalised in

1948 and in 1955 came under the control of the newly-formed British Transport Waterways. Despite the gradual decline in maintenance standards and the increasing competition from road haulage, the main line of the Shropshire Union still carried a considerable amount of commercial traffic until the 1960s. Right up to the end there were regular cargoes of chocolate carried between the Cadbury's factories at Knighton and Bourneville, oil from Stanlow refinery to Oldbury and aluminium from Walsall and Liverpool. Since the 1960s the canal has become increasingly popular as a cruising waterway, no doubt due to its attractive rural setting throughout much of its length.

A journey along the Shropshire Union Canal

We start our journey at Autherley Junction, the summit and southern end of the Shropshire Union Canal and junction with Brindley's Staffordshire & Worcestershire Canal. Half a mile to the south is Aldersley Junction where the Birmingham Canal Navigations meet the Staffs & Worcs. With its stop lock, toll office, cottages, stables and workshops Autherley, nicknamed 'Cut End', still retains the atmosphere of an important canal junction. The old canalside buildings, overlooking extensive moorings and boatyard, are now used by a boat-hire company and boat club. Proceeding in a north-westerly direction the canal skirts a housing estate that was built on the site of Wolverhampton Airport, opened in 1938, used as a flying school during World War II and closed in the 1950s. To the west of the canal is a massive sewage treatment work and soon the first of the old winding bridges is reached. These were built to enable a towing horse to cross from one side of the canal to the other without the need to unhitch the towing rope.

To the east of Bridge 4, where the canal enters open countryside, is the former Boulton & Paul aircraft factory where the Defiant fighter plane, the world's first with a power-operated gun turret, was built during World War II. From here to Nantwich the next 37 miles of the former Birmingham & Liverpool Junction Canal passes through a peaceful rural landscape, one of the reasons for its popularity as a cruising waterway. Between Bridges 5 and 6, where the canal briefly narrows, the modern concrete structure of the M54 bridge intrudes into

Above *Junction Bridge spans the entrance to the Shropshire Union Canal at Autherley Junction. Here, the summit and southerly end of the canal, is the junction with the Staffordshire & Worcestershire Canal.*

the tranquility. Two miles to the north of the motorway pollution the canal is framed by the attractively balustraded Avenue Bridge. The highly ornate bridge, carrying the private drive to nearby Chillington Hall, and a small wharf were erected by the canal builders in consideration for the Giffard family through whose parkland the canal passed. The 19th century house, approached along a long avenue of trees, stands in beautiful grounds that were landscaped by Capability Brown.

Passing through a wooded cutting the Shropshire Union Canal passes the picturesque village of Brewood, with its rows of attractive Georgian houses, market place and the popular canalside Bridge Inn.

Brewood Wharf, a short distance north of the village, was once a hive of industrial activity with lime kilns and gas works and is now home to a boat hire company.

Due to its 'cut-and-fill' construction the Shropshire Union marches across the Staffordshire and Cheshire landscape with great loping strides. Deep cuttings are followed in turn by massive embankments, affording the boat traveller magnificent vistas of the surrounding countryside. One mile north of Brewood the canal is carried over Watling Street (the A5), on the handsome cast iron Stretton Aqueduct built in 1832. To the west of the aqueduct is the 240-acre Belfide Reservoir, built as a feeder for the canal and doubled in size in 1836. It is now a bird sanctuary managed by the Royal Society for the Protection of Birds. Immediately north of the aqueduct is Stretton Wharf, built by the owners of nearby Stretton Hall, and the former Aqueduct Inn.

The Shropshire Union soon enters the long, steep-sided and tree-lined Lapley Wood Cutting, site of many spectacular landslips ever since the canal was built. Halfway along the cutting the Staffordshire Way long distance path, which has followed the canal towpath for the last few miles, veers off to the north east on its route to Penkridge. Soon after emerging from Lapley Wood the first lock for seven miles is reached at Wheaton Aston. To the north of the lock is Wheaton Aston Wharf with its former warehouses and the canalside Hartley Arms public house. North of the village is the site of a former World War II

Above *A narrowboat passes on its leisurely journey through a wooded cutting near Wood Eaton.*

Above *A narrowboat passes through the flood gate at the southern end of the massive Shelmore Embankment. Problems encountered during its construction seriously delayed the completion of the Birmingham & Liverpool Junction Canal.*

airfield, now a pig farm, where American pilots were trained by the RAF.

There now follows a long 18-mile pound until the next lock at Tyrley, the canal alternately burrowing through deep leafy cuttings and marching across high embankments, en route passing the villages of Church Easton, Gnossall, High Offley, Knighton and Cheswardine. South of Gnossall is the short Cowley Tunnel, originally planned to be much longer than its final 81yd length. During construction, engineers encountered serious faults in the surrounding rock and the tunnel is now approached through a deep rock cutting. Two canalside pubs in Gnossall, the Navigation and the Boat, conveniently provide sustenance for both towpath walkers and boat users. The disused railway bridge over the canal once carried the Stafford to Shrewsbury railway line, the only one built by the Shropshire Union Railway & Canal Company and opened in 1849. To the north of the village, the canal soars 60ft above the surrounding countryside on the massive Shelmore Embankment. The construction of this gigantic mile-long earthwork took over five years, during which time Thomas Telford had died, and seriously delayed the opening of the Birmingham & Liverpool Junction Canal.

At the northern end of the embankment is Norbury Junction where there is now a British Waterways yard, basin, boatyard, moorings and the popular canalside Junction Inn. This was once a bustling canal settlement and the junction with the Newport branch. Originally built as a branch to Shrewsbury, and thus the River Severn, only the section to just beyond Newport remained navigable and this was officially closed in 1944. North of Norbury the canal soon enters the deep, tree-lined and winding Grub Street Cutting whose southern end is framed by the unusual double-arched bridge. Excavated soil from this mile-long and 80ft-deep cutting was used in the construction of the giant Shelmore Embankment, one mile to the south.

Emerging from the cutting the Shropshire Union proceeds on its northerly course, soon reaching the isolated and atmospheric Anchor public house. This canalside inn, built at the same time as the canal, is a popular watering hole for boat users and towpath walkers. One mile to the north is yet another massive earthwork, the mile-long Shebdon

Left *The tranquil setting of Shebdon Wharf is mirrored in the still waters of the Shropshire Union Canal at the eastern end of Shebdon Embankment. Nestling below the embankment nearby is the popular Wharf Inn.*

Embankment, towering 50ft over the surrounding farms and farmland. The Wharf Inn, nestling in the shadows at the eastern end of the embankment, is yet another popular 19th century canalside pub. At the northern end, near the small village of Knighton, is a factory operated as a chocolate crumb processing unit for Cadbury's. Between 1911 and the early 1960s, the factory's output was transported by canal from Shebdon Wharf to Bourneville. Cadbury's were the first company to introduce their own fleet of motorised narrowboats which were used on this run until the early 1920s.

For the next five miles the Shropshire Union continues on a north westerly course to Tyrley Locks, for the most part passing through a tranquil easterly pocket of Shropshire farmland. This extremely rural stretch of canal, alternately passing through cuttings and across

Right *Restored former canal buildings make a fine sight at Tyrley Wharf. The Tyrley flight of five locks are the first since Autherley Junction and carry the Shropshire Union Canal down towards the valley of the River Tern.*

embankments, passes en route the disused Knighton feeder reservoir, several former coal wharves and the well patronised canalside Wharf Tavern at Goldstone Bridge. Between here and Tyrley is the deep and narrow Woodseaves Cutting. One of the major engineering feats on the canal, this fern and tree-lined cutting was excavated through a series of major rock faults to a depth of 90ft. Two magnificent arched bridges, the highest on the canal, complete the impression of travelling through a twilight world canyon.

Breaking forth into daylight again, the canal approaches Tyrley Wharf and the flight of five locks that starts to drop the Shropshire Union down towards sea level at Ellesmere Port. The wharf at Tyrley was once a bustling canal centre and the former wharf buildings, some built in a Tudor style by the owners of nearby Peatswood Estate, have been sympathetically restored in recent years. After descending the tree-lined flight of sandstone locks, the canal crosses the River Tern on an aqueduct and soon arrives at Market Drayton. Located on the eastern edge of this 17th century market town are boatyards, moorings, a large wharf, an imposing warehouse and, adjacent to Bridge 62, the Talbot canalside pub.

Leaving behind the clutter of Market Drayton wharves, the canal is soon out into open countryside again and its route is soon paralleled by the disused GWR railway line from Wellington to Nantwich. One mile before the next flight of locks at Adderley are reached, the boat user and towpath walker has to run the gauntlet of a shrieking ghost which is supposed to haunt the wooded Betton Cutting! The Adderley flight of five locks drops the canal a further 31ft towards the looming Cheshire Plain. Then, for the boat operator, there is only a brief respite of one-and-a-half miles before the Audlem flight of 15 locks has to be tackled. This closely grouped flight of locks drops the canal a further 93ft down towards the valley of the River Weaver. The picturesque canalside village of Audlem, overlooked by the 15th century church of St James, is well worth exploring. There are two popular and conveniently located canalside pubs in the village – the Bridge, appropriately situated adjacent to Audlem Bridge, and the Shroppie Fly, located in a converted warehouse on Audlem Wharf.

The final six-mile stretch of the former Birmingham & Liverpool Junction Canal from Audlem to Nantwich is characterised by the rich pasturelands of the Cheshire Plains, interspersed only by the two isolated Hack Green Locks. On the embanked approach to Nantwich Basin the canal crosses over the A51 road on an elegant cast iron aqueduct. The ancient town of Nantwich, once an important salt extraction centre, was badly damaged by fire in the 16th century but now contains many fine buildings. It was here that the narrow locked Birmingham & Liverpool Junction Canal joined with the wide locked Ellesmere & Chester Canal when the former opened in 1835. Nantwich Basin, formerly the terminus of the Ellesmere & Chester Canal, forms an arm off the main line of the canal and is overlooked by sympathetically restored former cheese warehouses. Its once busy

Above *An immaculately turned-out narrowboat approaches the Adderley flight of five locks.*

Above *A well-restored commercial narrowboat, painted in the colours of British Waterways, moored below Nantwich Junction bridge. Out of the picture to the left is Nantwich Basin, once the terminus of the Ellesmere & Chester Canal.*

commercial wharves are now home to boat hire companies with boatyards and moorings.

Northward from Nantwich, the character of the Shropshire Union Canal perceptibly changes. To the south the 'cut-and-fill' techniques used by Telford in the early 19th century created a very direct but narrow route to Autherley Junction. To the north, the more traditional construction methods used in the late 18th century, when the natural contours of the land were followed, have created a broader and winding waterway. One-and-a-half miles north of Nantwich lies Hurleston Junction, where the Llangollen Canal ascends up four narrow locks on its picturesque 46-mile journey to the valley of the River Dee at Llantisilio. Immediately to the west of the junction is Hurleston Reservoir, built to hold 85 million gallons of water that has flowed along the Llangollen Canal from the Dee. It was the use of the canal as an important source of water supply that fortunately saved it from closure in 1944 and it has since become one of the premier cruising waterways in the country.

Continuing on its north-westerly route the Shropshire Union leaves Hurleston Junction behind and after just over a mile reaches Barbridge and the junction with the Middlewich branch. This 10-mile waterway, opened in 1833 with four narrow locks, connects the Shropshire Union with the Trent & Mersey at Middlewich and is an important link in the Four Counties ring of cruising canals. Grouped close to this busy junction are two canalside pubs, the Barbridge Inn and the Jolly Tar, extensive moorings and a boatyard. Just beyond Barbridge Junction the Crewe to Chester railway line swings in from the east and accompanies the main line of the Shropshire Union on its 15-mile journey to Chester. Passing through Calveley, where the towpath changes sides, with its former rail-canal transshipment wharf and cheese warehouses, the canal arrives at the Bunbury twin-staircase locks. At Bunbury Wharf there are moorings, boatyard and a nice group of old canalside buildings, including former stables and warehouse, now utilised by a boat hire company.

North of Bunbury Wharf the canal winds its broad route between

Right *A narrowboat emerges from the Middlewich branch at Barbridge Junction. This 10-mile waterway connects the Shropshire Union with the Trent & Mersey at Middlewich.*

Above *The imposing staircase locks in the heart of the city of Chester are carved out of sandstone and drop the Shropshire Union a distance of 33ft down to Tower Wharf.*

wooded hills in the valley of the River Gowy, passing through picturesque Tilstone Lock with its former water mill, the two Beeston Locks and Wharton's Lock. Beeston Locks are unusual in that the first was constructed of stone while the other was rebuilt in 1828 using iron plates, made necessary due to the unstable nature of the underlying soil. At Wharton's Lock the canal has left the wooded valley behind and there are excellent views to the south of nearby Beeston Castle. From the lock, the Sandstone Trail long distance path provides access for the walker to the ruins of this 13th century castle, built on a hilltop 740ft above sea level. At Bate's Mill Bridge, a short distance west of the lock, is the popular Shady Oak canalside pub.

Still accompanied by the railway line and river, the Shropshire Union moves out into open pastureland in a level pound that stretches for the next eight miles to the outskirts of Chester. En route the canal passes the superbly restored Waverton Mill and the Old Trooper canalside pub before arriving at Christleton Lock. Nearby, Rowton Moor is the site of a major Civil War battle between Royalists and Parliamentarians in 1645. The picturesque village of Christleton is well worth a detour before descending the eleven locks to the River Dee at Chester. The final three miles into the city takes the canal through Greenfield Lock, Tarvin Road Lock, Chemistry Lock with its attractive canalside cottages, Hoole Lane Lock, through a red sandstone cutting overlooked by the city wall and King Charles' Tower and down through the three Northgate Staircase Locks. These imposing locks, dropping the canal a distance of 33ft, were excavated out of sandstone and take the Shropshire Union into the heart of this historic city. Below the locks is Tower Wharf, formerly the headquarters of the old canal company, where there are moorings and a boatyard. From Tower Wharf, three locks carry a short branch down to the tidal River Dee.

Many hours can be spent exploring this fascinating former Roman city with the most noteworthy sites being the old city walls and gates, King Charles' Tower, Roman remains, medieval streets and buildings, 11th century cathedral, castle and several fascinating museums.

The final part of our journey from Autherley Junction takes us along the Wirral Line of the former Ellesmere Canal, first passing under the stone viaduct that carries the Chester to Birkenhead railway line. The canal wends its way for 8½ miles across the flat landscape of the Wirral peninsula, passing under the M53 and M56 motorways near Stoak. On the approaches to Ellesmere Port the previously rural nature of most of the canal's route from Autherley changes to that of modern and ugly industry, dominated by belching chemical works and oil refineries. Soon, the wide expanse of the Mersey estuary comes into view as the Shropshire Union descends the last three locks into Ellesmere Port canal basin.

This once extensive and bustling canal port is linked to the Mersey by locks and part of the once-neglected docks complex has been turned into the widely acclaimed Boat Museum. Although Telford's fine old warehouse was destroyed by fire in 1970, his lighthouse, located at the entrance to the port, still stands as a lonely sentry overlooking the swirling currents of the tidal Mersey estuary.

The Boat Museum, Britain's premier canal museum, is located in the historic dock complex situated on the waterfront overlooking the Mersey Estuary. The dock with its Georgian and Victorian workshops, warehouses and stables, houses displays on working life on the canals, with information on canal development and local history together with a video presentation which sets the scene. Also moored on site are over 60 boats forming the world's largest collection of floating craft. Many of the craft can be boarded to explore the cabins where people lived in an area the size of a small hallway. Visitors can also experience a taste of life in the past with the 'Victorian' housekeeper in the period cottages, while a blacksmith is at work in the smithy and boats regularly work through the locks. The Pump House and Power Hall house a selection of engines, of which several are in daily operation. Boat trips are available through the locks or along the canal. A programme of events runs throughout the year, please telephone for details. (The Boat Museum, South Pier Road, Ellesmere Port, Cheshire L65 4FW. Telephone 0151 355 5017. Open daily April to October and Saturday to Wednesday from November to March.)

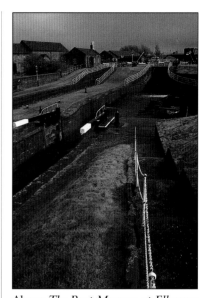

Above *The Boat Museum at Ellesmere Port, the northern terminus of the Shropshire Union Canal, is Britain's premier canal museum. The museum is located in the historic and superbly restored dock complex situated on the waterfront overlooking the Manchester Ship Canal and the Mersey Estuary.*

TRENT & MERSEY CANAL

ONE OF THE earliest canals to be built in the country, the Trent & Mersey was conceived as a link between the River Mersey and River Trent via The Potteries. The success of the Bridgewater Canal, opened in 1765 to provide an outlet for coal from the Duke of Bridgewater's mines at Worsley, gave an added impetus to promoters of the scheme. One of the principal promoters was Josiah Wedgwood, who saw the building of a canal through The Potteries as a valuable asset to industry in the region. The other promoters included Thomas Wheildon, Thomas Bentley, Earl Gower, Francis Egerton and Thomas Gilbert.

The Act of Parliament enabling the construction of the Trent & Mersey Canal, at an estimated cost of £100,000, was passed on 14th May 1766. The agreed route of the canal, 93½ miles in length, was from Shardlow on the navigable River Trent to Preston Brook, where it would link up with a new southerly extension to the Bridgewater Canal. Following his success with the latter canal, James Brindley was appointed Chief Engineer for the new scheme. Josiah Wedgwood cut the first sod at Burslem in July of the same year and construction work commenced simultaneously at Harecastle Tunnel and at Derwent Mouth on the River Trent. Initially, good progress was made. By 1771 the canal was open for traffic between the Trent and the southern outskirts of Stoke-on-Trent, linking with the Staffordshire & Worcestershire Canal at Great Haywood Junction. However, due to geological problems north of Stoke, progress slowed and on Brindley's death in 1772, Hugh Henshall was appointed Chief Engineer in his place. Apart from the incompleted Harecastle Tunnel, the canal was more or less complete by 1775. The 2926yd tunnel, the major

Left The narrowboat Water Witch emerges from the northern portal of Harecastle Tunnel. Completed in 1827 to overcome a notorious bottleneck, this is the second of the tunnels to be built at Harecastle. Until the original bore was closed in 1918 due to mining subsidence, each tunnel operated as a one-way route. The colour of the water on this part of the Trent & Mersey is permanently stained orange due to the presence of iron in the soil.

Above Canalside cottages overlook the locks at Fradley Junction where the Coventry Canal meets the Trent & Mersey. Designed as a through route between Coventry and the Trent & Mersey Canal and to carry coal from Bedworth to Coventry, but dogged by financial problems, the 38-mile Coventry Canal was opened in stages between 1769 and 1790.

engineering feature on the Trent & Mersey, took another two years to complete and so the complete route with 76 locks was not opened throughout until May 1777, at a final cost of nearly £300,000 – three times the original estimate!

The newly opened canal was an immediate success and brought great prosperity to the region, especially The Potteries – thus vindicating Josiah Wedgwood's original confidence in the scheme. Vast amounts of raw materials were able to be conveyed to the growing pottery industry, china clay and flint was brought in by sea to the Mersey and then transported by narrow boat along the canal. In addition to locally mined coal, manufactured goods, such as china, earthenware, bricks and tiles were carried to the growing industrialised cities of England. Following on the heels of this success the Trent & Mersey soon opened up several branches from its main line, eventually being physically linked to many other canals in the region – earning the title of Grand Trunk Canal.

The canal, serving the vast industrial area of the Potteries, was soon stretched to capacity and the long, single-bore Harecastle Tunnel

Right *The northern portal of the original Harecastle Tunnel, closed due to subsidence in 1918.*

became a major bottleneck. As there was no towpath provided in the tunnel, boats had to be 'legged' through by men lying on their backs. Thomas Telford was contracted to build a second parallel tunnel with a towpath and this was opened in 1827, each tunnel then being one-way only. This situation ended when the original tunnel had to be closed this century due to mining subsidence. Electric tugs were introduced in 1914 to speed up freight movement through the tunnel and these continued to operate until the early 1950s.

Until the 1830s the canal traded very profitably, the first dividend of 5% was paid to shareholders as early as 1784 and by 1821 had increased to 75%. Similarly, share prices which were valued at £200 in 1784 were changing hands for £2400 by 1824. However, by 1835 the Railway Age was dawning and soon the profitability of the Trent & Mersey was being threatened. The canal company responded by cutting toll charges but by 1846 it became clear that the neighbouring North Staffordshire Railway would take away much of its trade. The Trent & Mersey management took a pragmatic approach over this threat, agreeing a takeover by the NSR in January 1847. The new owners took a reasonably paternalistic attitude towards its new acquisition and maintenance standards were kept at an acceptable level until the 1870s.

As late as the 1870s a new and unusual link with the Trent & Mersey was proposed by the trustees of the River Weaver Navigation. At Anderton the Weaver flowed close to, but 50ft below, the canal – tantalising close but frustrating because there was no physical connection. The Anderton Lift, designed by Leader Williams, was built in 1875 to lift boats the 50ft between the river and canal. Originally the hydraulic rams that raised and lowered the two massive water-filled caissons were operated by steam power. In 1903 the lift was modernised and steam power was replaced by electricity. In 1982 it was closed due to structural faults and funding is currently awaited to retore it to full working order.

Inevitably though, trade did inexorably slip away from canal to railway and by 1921, when the London Midland & Scottish Railway took over the NSR and thus the canal, the writing was definitely on the

Above *Until 1982 the Anderton Boat Lift carried barges down from the Trent & Mersey to the River Weaver. Since then the lift has been out of use and a trust is currently raising funds to restore and manage this wonder of the canal world.*

Above This former 18th century mill at Shardlow, complete with central arch to enable boats to load, is now a smart restaurant and inn.

wall for the T&M. Commercial traffic continued to decline and nationalisation in 1948 did nothing to reverse this trend. To give some idea of this decline, over one million tons of goods were carried on the T&M at the turn of the century but this had shrunk to 186,000 tons by 1946 and to 24,000 tons by 1959. By the 1960s commercial traffic had virtually disappeared but today the canal, passing as it does through both delightful countryside and the ghosts of England's industrial heritage, provides a fascinating route for leisure cruisers on the Cheshire Ring of canals.

A journey along the Trent & Mersey Canal

The River Trent is navigable as far inland as Cavendish Bridge, close to the village of Shardlow in Derbyshire. The Trent & Mersey Canal commences its 93½-mile journey at Derwent Mouth, on a bend of the River Trent and at the confluence of the River Derwent, one mile east of Shardlow. The section of canal between here and Horninglow and the northern section between Preston Brook and Middlewich were built to accommodate wide beam river barges. The locks in these two sections are 14ft wide compared to the 7ft wide locks of the central section between Horninglow and Middlewich. Between Derwent Mouth and Shardlow is the solitary Derwent Mouth Lock and just beyond, adjacent to Bridge 2, are the Malt Shovel and New Inn canalside pubs. Shardlow is an excellently preserved example of a late-18th century canal village with restored warehouses, boatyards, boat hire facilities, moorings and the popular Navigation canalside pub. The Trent & Mersey Canal leaves Shardlow behind, passing through open pastureland with the meandering River Trent never far away to the south east. The isolated Aston Lock, overlooked by a diminutive arched bridge, precedes the railway bridge that carried the former Midland Railway line from Trent Junction to Burton-upon-Trent. Immediately after the railway bridge is Weston Lock, lifting the canal a height of 11ft, and the nearby village of Weston-upon-Trent with its fine 14th century hilltop church. Wooded hills close in as the River Trent meanders in beside the canal at Cliff Wood where, hidden amongst the trees, there is a Ukrainian farming settlement. Parting company with

Left *Seen under a threatening sky, a short arm providing moorings is all that remains of the Derby Canal at Swarkestone.*

the river again, the canal swings round a bend and approaches Swarkestone Lock, raising the canal a further 11ft. A short arm at Swarkestone, now used as moorings, is all that remains of the old Derby Canal.

The Derby Canal was engineered by Benjamin Outram and opened in 1796. It linked the Erewash Canal at Sandiacre, via Derby, with the Trent & Mersey Canal at Swarkestone, a total of 14½ miles. A branch to Little Eaton, just over 3 miles in length, linked with the tramway which served mines and works in and around Denby. Coal was transported in boxes, forerunners of modern containers, which were transshipped by crane to the barges at Little Eaton. Due to the advent of new railway lines traffic soon began to decline, coal traffic ceasing in 1908 and by 1927 other commercial traffic had virtually ceased. The whole canal had been abandoned by 1964.

The freight-only railway line from Trent Junction crosses the canal again at Swarkestone and keeps company with it all the way into Burton-upon-Trent. West of Swarkestone, the Trent & Mersey follows a dead-straight line for two-and-a-half miles as far as Stenson Lock. This is the last wide-beam lock on the southern section of the canal, allowing river barges to travel as far as Horninglow Wharf near Burton-upon-Trent. Adjacent to the 12ft-deep lock is a marina with boatyard and moorings, and the Bubble Inn canalside pub. A short distance to the west of the lock, the canal dives under the main Derby to Birmingham railway line before making a sharp left-hand turn to the village of Findern and the Greyhound canalside pub. Just across the railway line is Willington Power Station and, beyond, the meandering River Trent.

South west of Findern, the Trent & Mersey Canal dives under yet another railway bridge – this one carries the former North Staffordshire Railway's line to Stoke-on-Trent which branches off the main line at this point – and then winds its way past the little village of Willington. The village is a veritable drinker's paradise with its three closely-grouped canalside pubs – the Green Man, the Rising Sun and the Green Dragon. Soon, the canal and railway line are joined from the west by the busy A38 trunk road, all keeping company with one another on the next nine miles to Barton-under-Needwood.

On the outskirts of Burton a fine nine-arched stone aqueduct carries the canal over the River Dove. Approaching the famous brewing town, the canal passes through the industrialised outskirts, passing Horninglow Wharf with the smell of hops and malt pervading the air. Horninglow Wharf was the furthest point on the southern section of the canal that wide-beam river barges could reach. Close to the wharf is the Bass Museum, opened in 1977, housed in 19th century Bass brewery buildings. Just beyond the wharf is Dallow Lane Lock, the first of the narrow locks on the central section to Middlewich. Three-quarters of a mile further on, in the south western outskirts of the town, is the restored Shobnall Basin where there is now a boatyard and moorings. The basin is all that remains of the Shobnall Branch which, until the coming of railways, served the local breweries.

Left Set on a low hill, Wychnor Church overlooks peaceful moorings on the Trent & Mersey Canal.

Now out into open countryside, the Trent & Mersey passes under the A38 trunk road, through the solitary Branston Lock to Branston Bridge and the canalside Bridge public house. Continuing in a south-westerly direction and still keeping company with the main road and railway, the canal climbs up through Tatenhill Lock, past flooded gravel pits to arrive at Barton Lock and yet another canalside pub – the Bartons Turn. The roar of traffic on the adjacent A38 dual carriageway contrasts greatly with the leisurely progress of narrowboats passing through the lock. The road keeps company for another one-and-a-half miles to Wychnor Lock, where the canal heads off into more peaceful surroundings past the charming little Wychnor Church. Just before the picturesque village of Alrewas, the meandering River Trent briefly joins company with the canal before heading off in a westerly direction at Alrewas Lock. The village itself is well worth exploring with its pretty timbered and thatched cottages, 14th century church and three pubs. After

Left Gardens run down to the canal bank in the picturesque village of Alrewas.

meandering through the village, the Trent & Mersey passes through Bagnall Lock and heads out into open countryside, passing through the isolated Common Lock, towards Fradley Junction. On the approach to this junction with the Coventry Canal, the canal passes through the closely spaced Hunts Lock, Keepers Lock and Junction Lock.

Fradley Junction is still an important and busy canal junction with moorings, boat hire company, a boatyard and the popular Swan canalside boatman's inn.

Leaving Fradley Junction behind, the Trent & Mersey climbs up through the closely spaced Middle Lock and Shade House Lock and out into wooded countryside, then executes a sharp bend to take a north-westerly course through lonely Woodend Lock. From here, the canal enters a 10-mile pound as far as Colwich. At Handsacre, where the electrified Euston to Glasgow railway line and the River Trent briefly join company with the canal, the Crown canalside pub offers yet another refreshment opportunity for the walker or boat user. The neighbouring village of Armitage, famous for its manufacture of WCs, was, until the early 1970s, the site of a short canal tunnel. The tunnel, removed at that time due to subsidence, was the first in Britain to be built with a towpath. Near to the site of the tunnel, now replaced by a cutting and road bridge, is the Plum Pudding canalside pub. To the south of the canal is Spode House and Hawkesyard Priory, built by the pottery family of the same name, while at Bridge 62 is the Ash Tree canalside pub. The approaches to the rather dull town of Rugeley are dominated by Lea Hall Colliery and the cooling towers of Rugeley Power Station.

One mile to the north of Rugeley, the Trent & Mersey executes an S-bend, crossing over the River Trent on a magnificent stone aqueduct, before being briefly accompanied again by the electrified railway line. The former royal hunting forest of Cannock Chase, now a 7000-acre area of outstanding natural beauty, lies across the river valley to the west. Still keeping close company with the River Trent the canal wends its way through a lush valley, passing the classical facade of Bishton Hall and the Wolseley Arms public house at nearby Wolseley Bridge. Passing

Above British Waterways offices are located in attractively restored canal wharf buildings at Fradley Junction where the Coventry Canal meets the Trent & Mersey. Today, the Coventry Canal is still an important link in the Midlands and its pleasant, mainly rural route is increasingly used by pleasure boats. Fradley Junction is still an important and busy canal junction with moorings, a boatyard and the popular Swan canalside boatman's inn.

through Colwich Lock, located close to a busy railway junction, the canal continues through a tranquil wooded valley and soon skirts the parkland of nearby Shugborough Hall. The Hall, formerly the home of the Earl of Lichfield and now owned by the National Trust, was built at the end of the 17th century and has been restored to its former glory. The landscaped parkland is decorated with many Grecian stone monuments sculpted by the 18th-century artist, James Stuart. The impressive house is leased by Staffordshire County Council as the Museum of Staffordshire Life and access from the canal is via the bridge adjacent to Haywood Lock.

Haywood Lock is picturesquely sandwiched in a conservation area between the confluence of the Rivers Sow and Trent to the west, and the former North Staffordshire Railway line to Stoke-on-Trent and the village of Great Haywood to the east. Within the village are pretty former estate cottages, an ancient packhorse bridge, two churches and two pubs. A short distance north of the lock is Great Haywood Junction where the Staffordshire & Worcestershire Canal emerges under a wide brick roving bridge to join the Trent & Mersey.

Right Lucy Ginger *heads for Haywood Lock as the Trent & Mersey skirts the parkland of Shugborough Hall. The cast iron bridge in the distance was built to carry a private drive across the canal to the hall.*

The Staffordshire & Worcestershire Canal was designed by James Brindley as part of a canal system to link the Rivers Severn, Trent, Thames and Mersey. Its opening in 1772 created a new canal town at Stourport-on-Severn, where goods were transshipped from canal narrow boats to the larger Severn trows. The opening of the 46-mile canal gave direct access from Bristol and Gloucester, via the River Severn, to the Midlands and the Potteries. Although the canal soon faced competition from the Worcester & Birmingham and Birminghan & Liverpool Junction Canals, opened in 1815 and 1835 respectively, the company remained profitable to the end of the 19th century. Unlike most of its counterparts the Staffordshire & Worcestershire never sold out to a railway company and remained totally independent until nationalisation in 1947, but by then commercial traffic had virtually disappeared. The complete section of canal in Staffordshire was made a Conservation Area in 1978. Despite the passage of years the canal still retains an atmosphere of bygone days, due mainly to the total lack of modernisation, and because of this and its delightful rural setting it is now very popular for cruising.

Left *An attractive towing path bridge guards the entrance to the Staffordshire & Worcestershire Canal at Great Haywood Junction.*

Above The still waters of the Trent & Mersey reflect these quiet moorings near Lock 29 in the town of Stone.

Great Haywood Junction and its old warehouses, boatyard and moorings are soon left behind as the Trent & Mersey, still sandwiched between the River Trent and railway, continues on its north-westerly course. As the valley opens out, the canal climbs up through Hoo Mill Lock, then passes the Coach & Horses canalside pub at Bridge 77. To the west is Ingestre Hall, once the home of the Earl of Shrewsbury and rebuilt in the 19th century after a fire. It is now an arts centre set in parkland that was designed by Capability Brown. Continuing up the valley of the Trent, the canal snakes its way up through Weston Lock and past the busy roadside village of Weston where the Saracen's Head is a convenient canalside pub. Between Weston and Sandon the meandering River Trent and electrified railway line squeeze in alongside the canal, bordered to the north-east by the grounds of Sandon Park. The 19th-century house was once the seat of the Earl of Harrowby and in the grounds is the 75ft-high Pitt's Column, graced by a statue of William Pitt the Younger.

Sandon Lock, lifting the canal a height of 10ft, is located to the south of the estate village where the Dog & Doublet public house is sandwiched between the railway line and busy A51 road. From Sandon, a picturesque two-and-a-half mile pound takes the Trent & Mersey to Aston Lock followed by a further one-and-a-half mile pound to the first of the Stone flight of locks. These four closely grouped locks lift the canal a further 39ft towards the summit at Etruria. The old town of Stone was once the headquarters of the Trent & Mersey Canal Company and, as such, still has an extensive boatyard containing drydocks for boatbuilding and maintenance of leisure craft. There are several pubs in Stone that are adjacent or close to the canal, but specific mention must be made of the Star – an old canal pub located on the towpath close to the bottom lock.

As the canal leaves the town behind, it parts company with the River Trent and executes a sharp turn to the north. Immediately ahead are the Meaford flight of four locks which lift the canal a further 32ft. To overcome congestion at this location, a flight of three staircase locks was replaced in the 1830s by the lower three locks that are in use today. At the top lock the former North Staffordshire Railway main line joins company with the canal again for the next seven miles to Stoke-on-Trent.

Accompanied by the railway line, the Trent & Mersey continues on its northerly route through the Staffordshire landscape, passing Meaford Power Station and the Plume of Feathers canalside pub at Barlaston. At Oldroad Bridge, just prior to Trentham Lock, a stop can be made to visit the Wedgwood Museum and Visitor Centre. This is located in the world famous Wedgwood Pottery factory, built in 1940 to replace the original factory at Etruria. Josiah Wedgwood, the chief promoter of the Trent & Mersey Canal, started the business in 1759 and since then it has become one of the largest and most successful china and pottery manufacturers in the world.

Left Built to last, these solid Victorian brewery buildings at Stone were once served by canal boat.

Above A narrowboat descends through the locks at Etruria. Close by is the junction with the Caldon Canal and the restored Shirley's Bone Mill. A statue of James Brindley has been erected close to the junction between the two canals.

North of Oldroad Bridge, Trentham Lock lifts the canal a further 12ft towards the summit then passes Hemheath Bridge where the Trentham Inn is another conveniently situated canalside pub. The Trent & Mersey is now entering the industrial outskirts of Stoke-on-Trent, still an important centre of the pottery industry. Although the industry has now been modernised, there are still ghosts of the past in the shape of several of the remarkable brick bottle kilns that have fortunately been preserved. The present day town of Stoke-on-Trent was formed of six separate towns, Burslem, Fenton, Hanley, Longton, Stoke and Tunstall, in 1910. The area, known as The Potteries, has been an important centre for pottery production since Roman times. The opening of the canal in 1777 enabled the industry to expand and brought much prosperity to the area, thus vindicating Josiah Wedgwood's original confidence in the scheme. Vast amounts of raw materials were able to be conveyed to the growing pottery industry, china clay and flint was brought in by sea to the Mersey and then transported by narrow boat along the canal. In addition to locally mined coal, manufactured goods, such as china, earthenware, bricks and tiles were carried to the growing industrialised cities of England. Stoke-on-Trent contains several museums that are worth visiting, including the City Museum & Art Gallery with its superb collection of ceramics, the Spode Museum and the Arnold Bennett Museum.

Starting close to Stoke-on-Trent railway station, the Stoke flight of five locks lifts the Trent & Mersey a further 50ft to its summit pound which starts at Etruria. It was here that Josiah Wedgwood built his famous canalside factory and industrial village in 1768. Production of Wedgwood china and pottery was moved to Barlaston in 1940 and the old factory was sadly demolished in 1968 to make way for a new road scheme. Etruria is also where the delightful Caldon Canal starts its journey to the picturesque Churnet Valley. Opposite the junction is a recently erected statue of James Brindley, the Chief Engineer of the Trent & Mersey until his death in 1772.

The Main Line of the Caldon Canal, from Etruria to Froghall, was opened in 1779 as a 17½-mile branch of the Trent & Mersey Canal and was primarily built to transport limestone from quarries at Caldon Low, linked to the canal via a horse-drawn tramway. The 2½-mile Leek Branch, involving a flyover junction at Hazlehurst, was opened in 1801 and carries water for the Trent & Mersey Canal from nearby Rudyard Lake. A further branch from Froghall to Uttoxeter was opened in 1811. The North Staffordshire Railway purchased the Trent & Mersey Canal Company, including the Caldon Canal, in 1846 and promptly closed the Froghall to Uttoxeter branch using part of its route for a new railway line. With the opening of more railway lines the canal's fortunes slumped and by 1960 it had become very overgrown and silted up. A group of canal preservationists put pressure on the local authorities and with much volunteer help the canal was reopened to boats in 1974. The route today, firstly through the Potteries industrial landscape around Hanley, runs through extremely attractive countryside with much to interest both the walker and boatman.

The summit level pound of the Trent & Mersey Canal takes the waterway through the industrial landscape of Etruria, past the landscaped site of the 1986 National Garden Festival, Burslem, Longport and Tunstall before diving into the southern portal of the 2897yd Harecastle Tunnel. The original tunnel was the major engineering feature on the canal and took 11 years to build. As there was no towpath provided, boats had to be 'legged' through by men lying on their backs – up to three hours was allowed for this backbreaking journey! The canal, serving the vast industrial area of the Potteries, was soon stretched to capacity and the tunnel became a major bottleneck. Thomas Telford was contracted to build a second parallel tunnel and this was opened in 1827 at a cost of over £100,000, each tunnel then being one-way only. This situation ended when the original tunnel had to be closed in 1918 due to mining subsidence. Electric tugs, obtaining power from an overhead wire, were introduced in 1914 to speed up freight movement through the tunnel and these continued to operate until the early 1950s. Following the abandonment of the electric tug service a system of forced ventilation was introduced in 1954 to enable diesel-powered boats to transit the tunnel under their own power.

Left Sir Alisander *emerges into daylight after passing through the 2897yd Harecastle Tunnel. A British Waterways maintenance boat is moored alongside. The water is stained orange due to the presence of iron in the soil.*

Telford's Tunnel also suffered from mining subsidence and had to be closed for four years during the 1970s for major repairs.

A major feature at the northern portal of the Harecastle Tunnel is the water that is permanently stained orange by the presence of iron in the soil. Emerging from the tunnel, the canal passes through the town of Kidsgrove and approaches the unusual Hardings Wood Junction where the Macclesfield Canal leaves the main line, crossing it on Red Bull Aqueduct. Immediately after the junction is the first of the Red Bull flight of six locks that drop the Trent & Mersey beneath the aqueduct. There are several boatyards in this area and canalside pubs include the appropriately named Red Bull and the Blue Bell and Tavern, both of these being located close to the junction of the two canals.

Conceived, rather late in the day, as a direct link between Manchester and the Midlands the 28-mile Macclesfield Canal was surveyed by Thomas Telford and engineered by William Crosley. It was opened in 1831, more than 50 years after the more or less parallel Trent & Mersey Canal, and, despite early competition from the railways and the Trent & Mersey, it was a fairly successful commercial carrier into the early part of the 20th century. The canal, along with the Ashton and the Peak Forest, was taken over in 1846 by the predecessor to the Great Central Railway. Decline in traffic eventually set in and had completely ceased by 1960. However it was never actually closed and with the increased interest in canals as leisure amenities it has seen an upsurge in traffic from leisure boats using the picturesque canal as an important section of the 100-mile Cheshire Ring of waterways.

Leaving the summit pound and the Red Bull flight of locks behind, the Trent & Mersey moves out into gently rolling countryside and follows a sharp S-bend around the hilltop village of Church Lawton. There now follows a very heavily locked section of canal with each lock being arranged with a duplicate alongside. Immediately ahead are the three Hall's Locks followed by the Lawton Treble Locks, together dropping the canal a further 56ft down towards the Cheshire Plain.

Above *Viewed from Red Bull aqueduct, where the Macclesfield Canal crosses the Trent & Mersey, a narrowboat works through the flight of paired narrow locks.*

Round the next bend, close to the small village of Rode Heath, are the two Thurlwood Locks and the conveniently located Broughton Arms canalside public house. Crossing Chells Hill Aqueduct the canal drops down through the two Pierpoint locks, the two Hassall Green locks and under the M6 motorway to arrive at the top of the Wheelock flight of eight paired locks. At Malkins Bank, halfway down the flight, is a boatyard and a pretty row of terraced cottages. The small village of Wheelock, set on the outskirts of the town of Sandbach, lies at the bottom of the flight and with its three canalside pubs – Nags Head, Cheshire Cheese and Commercial – is a useful resting place after the exhaustions of locking down from Kidsgrove.

The Trent & Mersey is now entering an area of salt extraction and for years has been prone to subsidence caused by centuries of rock salt mining and brine pumping. On the approaches to the town of Middlewich, the centre of the salt industry, the canal drops down a further 29ft through the Booth Lane flight of three locks before passing several large salt works. At the isolated Rumps Lock, alongside the busy

Right *A graceful brick bridge takes the towpath over the entrance to a small arm at Malkins Bank, close to the village of Wheelock.*

A533 road, the Kinderton Arms is a useful canalside pub. As the canal enters the town it passes through Kings Lock, immediately followed by the junction with the Middlewich Branch of the Shropshire Union Canal. This 10-mile branch was not opened from Barbridge Junction until 1833 and now provides a useful link for leisure craft with the Shropshire Union and thence the Llangollen Canal. Past the junction, the T&M drops down the Middlewich flight of three locks, passing several boatyards before arriving at the first of the wide beam locks of the northern section. Much of the locally mined salt was once transported by canal and, until the narrowing of Croxton Aqueduct some years ago, wide beam barges could travel all the way from the centre of Middlewich to Manchester. The Big Lock, Newton Brewery Inn and Kings Lock are all conveniently located canalside pubs in the town.

There now follows a lock-free pound to Preston Brook at the northern end of the Trent & Mersey. North of Middlewich the canal is carried over the River Dane on Croxton Aqueduct, now restricted to

Left *Working a narrowboat through Kings Lock, Middlewich. To quench the thirst, the nearby pub offers a good variety of liquid refreshments. In the distance, the towpath bridge marks the junction with the Middlewich branch of the Shropshire Union Canal.*

Above *A narrowboat prepares to enter the eastern portal of 572yd Barnton Tunnel. At the western end, the canal emerges into a short, tree-lined cutting before burrowing into the shorter Saltersford Tunnel.*

narrow beam boats, and into the picturesque Dane Valley where it skirts the grounds of Bostock Hall. Leaving the meandering River Dane behind, the Trent & Mersey snakes round the parkland of Whatcroft Hall and then enters an area of lagoons caused by subsidence of underground salt mines. The canal soon passes the outskirts of the town of Northwich, still an important centre for the salt industry and strategically located on the navigable River Weaver.

The River Weaver has been an important waterway since the 17th century when locally mined salt was carried by sailing barges. Due to the expansion of this industry improvements were made by 1732 to enable barges to navigate the 20 miles as far as Winsford. Traffic steadily increased, not only from salt but also coal and clay for the Potteries. After the opening of the Trent & Mersey Canal a transshipment point with the Weaver was established at Anderton and in 1875 the famous Anderton Lift was opened enabling barges to be raised or lowered between the two waterways. Further improvements, such as enlarging the locks and canalising sections, were made to the Weaver in the 19th century, and the Weston Canal was built to the new docks at Weston Point in 1806. The opening of the Manchester Ship Canal in 1890 further improved trade and today 1000-ton vessels still carry cargo for the local chemical industries.

Continuing on its level pound, the Trent & Mersey passes through the famous salt mining village of Marston beneath which are a labyrinth of caves formed by centuries of salt extraction and brine pumping. In their wake, the vast workings have brought about much subsidence to buildings and the canal in the area. One section of canal had to be rerouted in the 1950s when part of the original route disappeared into a large hole in the ground. As the River Weaver draws ever closer the enormous and unique steel structure of the Anderton Boat Lift comes into view.

Designed by the Chief Engineer of the River Weaver Navigation, Leader Williams, this unique boat lift was built in 1875 to connect the Trent & Mersey Canal with the River Weaver. Two massive water-filled caissons, originally operated by hydraulic rams, raised or lowered canal boats a distance of 50ft between canal and river. In 1908 the lift was modernised and steam power was replaced by electricity. Currently awaiting restoration, it remains one of the great wonders of the canal world. Clinging to the hillside high above the Weaver, the Trent & Mersey passes through the 572yd Barnton Tunnel, emerging high above Saltersford Locks before plunging into the shorter Saltersford Tunnel. Leaving the tunnel behind, the canal continues on its north-westerly route along the side of a wooded hillside above the river. The river and canal part company on the final stretch through woodland to Preston Brook Tunnel. The northern end of the crooked 1239yd-long tunnel marks the boundary between the Trent & Mersey and the Bridgewater Canal. No towpath was provided in the tunnel so in the days of horse-drawn boats the horse had to follow a path over the hill while the boat was 'legged' through.

Left *Currently awaiting funds to restore it to use, the Anderton Boat Lift is overlooked by industrial works lining the southern bank of the River Weaver.*

OXFORD CANAL

Above *Looking south from inside Newbold Tunnel. Built during the modernisation of the Oxford Canal in the 1830s, the 250yd tunnel boasts a towpath on both sides, although only one of them is currently accessible. The canal emerges into a heavily wooded cutting close to the Boat and Barley Mow pubs.*

As early as the 17th century there were proposals to make the River Cherwell navigable between Banbury and Oxford, thus linking London, via the River Thames to this important agricultural region. By 1768 the Coventry Canal was already being built and James Brindley was commissioned to survey and report on the feasibility of a new canal to link it to Oxford. This would effectively provide an outlet between the growing industrial Midlands, the collieries served by the Coventry Canal and London, via the River Thames.

The promotors of the proposed Oxford Canal gained considerable support and the relevant Act of Parliament was passed in April 1769. The estimated cost of the canal was £150,000 and shares in the new enterprise were soon snapped up. James Brindley was appointed Chief Engineer but within a few months he had fallen out with the Company to such an extent that he offered to resign. Ruffled feathers were soon smoothed and Brindley never carried out his threat. Construction work on the winding, contour-hugging route progressed so that by 1771 ten miles were open to traffic and the Company began taking an income. However, due to the structuring of tolls as laid down in the Act of Parliament, the site of the junction with the Coventry Canal was a continual problem. It was not until 1777 that this was finally resolved and the outcome at the time degenerated into farce. The final solution agreed between the two companies meant that the two canals ran closely parallel for over a mile, forming a physical junction at Longford, thus increasing the mileage and tolls charged for goods being carried. This situation lasted until 1785 when a more practical junction between the two canals was opened at Hawkesbury.

Brindley had died in 1772 and his assistant, Samual Simcock was appointed in his place. By 1774 the canal was completed as far as Napton and by 1778 had reached Banbury. Due to the Coventry Canal not being completed to its junction with the Birmingham Canals at

Left *The heavily locked section of the Oxford Canal at Napton. This beautiful part of Warwickshire is dominated by the restored windmill on the summit of 400ft-high Napton Hill. Clinging to the side of the hill is the village of Napton with its brickworks and 13th century church. The Oxford Canal winds round the base of the hill to Napton Junction where the Grand Union Canal swings off in a north-westerly direction towards Warwick and Birmingham.*

Fazeley, the hoped-for through traffic to the Oxford Canal did not materialise and construction work stopped at Banbury. It was not until 1785, when the Coventry Canal's plans for completion became clear, that the Oxford Canal Company decided to press ahead with the building of the rest of the canal from Banbury to Oxford. This contour-hugging route, closely following (and in several places utilising) the meandering course of the River Cherwell, was completed in January 1790. The total cost of the 91-mile canal from Longford to Oxford, including 42 locks, was over £300,000. By July of that year the Coventry Canal was completed to Fazeley where it formed a junction with the Birmingham & Fazeley Canal. For the first time there was now a continuous canal and river system that linked the Mersey, Trent, Severn and Thames – the Oxford Canal flourished and patient

Right *A tranquil scene on the Oxford Canal at the picturesque village of Cropredy, site of a battle fought in the Civil War. Just beyond the bridge is Cropredy Lock where the River Cherwell first accompanies the canal for the rest of its journey to the outskirts of Oxford.*

shareholders were being rewarded with dividends of 11% by 1801.

Until 1805, the Oxford Canal was part of the only direct route between London and Birmingham. In that year the Grand Junction Canal was completed, reducing the distance that goods had to be carried between those two cities by 60 miles. The Warwick & Birmingham and Warwick & Napton Canals formed a junction with the Oxford Canal at Napton Junction, whilst the Grand Junction started its route to London at Braunston, also on the Oxford Canal. Naturally, the Oxford Canal lost most of its through traffic to this shorter route but compensation, in the shape of extortionate tolls charged between Napton and Braunston, kept the company's finances buoyant for many years – between 1812 and 1841 the dividend to shareholders never fell below 30%.

The original section of the canal from Hawkesbury Junction to Wolfhamcote followed an extremely tortuous and winding route. In 1829 a plan to shorten this section by 13½ miles was proposed. The Act of Parliament authorising this major work at an estimated cost of £130,000 was passed in 1831 and construction, under the watchful eye of William Cubitt, started immediately. Brindley's meandering route was straightened out and by 1834 this virtually new canal was completed and for a few years the company continued to prosper. However, competition from the new railways was only just round the corner.

Soon, both the Great Western and the London & North Western Railways were extending their tentacles into the area served by the Oxford Canal. As with other canal companies up and down the country, the Oxford fought back by lowering toll charges. Not surprisingly, receipts from tolls started falling but, partly due to good management, dividends to shareholders never dropped below 4½% – this low point being reached in 1899 and as late as 1938 the dividend had climbed back to 8%.

Commercial traffic on the southern section between Napton and Oxford had virtually disappeared by the time the Oxford Canal was nationalised in 1948. The northern section continued to carry coal

Above *An ornate cast iron bridge transfers the towpath from one side to the other at Fenny Compton 'Tunnel'. This long and steep-sided rock cutting was originally two tunnels which were opened up in 1870 to relieve a notorious bottleneck on the Oxford Canal.*

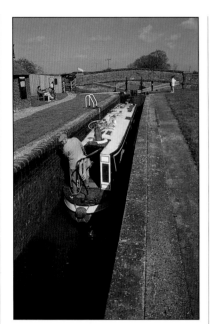

Above A narrow boat negotiates the first of the Napton flight of nine locks at Marston Dole. The lock marks the end of an 11-mile contour-hugging summit pound that meanders through tranquil countryside on the Warwickshire/Oxfordshire border.

until the late 1960s when this traffic was lost to road and rail. Since then this canal has seen a tremendous upsurge in use by leisure craft, its popularity no doubt greatly assisted by its picturesque and meandering rural route particularly on the southern section from Napton to Oxford.

A journey along the Oxford Canal

Our journey along the Oxford Canal starts at Hawkesbury Junction, also known as Sutton Stop, where it joins the Coventry Canal. Sutton was the surname of a family of toll-keepers who held this post for nearly 70 years during the 19th century. A stop-lock, with a drop of only 6in, protects the waters of the Oxford from the Coventry. The original and time-wasting junction with the Coventry Canal was once located at Longford, about one mile to the south-west on the Coventry Canal. Today, this former canal settlement on the outskirts of Coventry features attractive cast-iron bridges and the popular Greyhound canalside public house.

Until 1834, the northern section of the Oxford Canal from Hawkesbury Junction to Wolfhamcote followed a meandering course totalling 38 miles. However, in that year a modernisation programme to widen and straighten this section of canal was completed, thus reducing the mileage by 13½ miles. Now, this northern section is characterised by many glimpses of the original route, with cast-iron tow-path bridges and embankments giving clues as to where the newer, straighter route cut across the old loops.

Leaving Hawkesbury Junction, the Oxford Canal follows a meandering course to Tusses Bridge and the canalside Elephant & Castle public house, where the M6 motorway parallels a straightened section of the canal for the next mile. The remains of the Wyken Colliery branch, now truncated by the motorway, provides moorings for leisure craft. At Stone Bridge the canal veers away to the east, parting company with the fumes and noise of the M6, and into open countryside. Soon passing under the M69 motorway, the canal follows a meandering course to the small village of Ansty where the Rose &

Castle is a conveniently located public house. A short distance to the east of Ansty the electrified Crewe to Rugby railway line comes in to accompany the canal for the next 2½ miles. The Oxford Canal follows its 'newly straightened' course – the elegant cast-iron towpath bridges marking the abandoned loops of the original course – on embankments, through cuttings and passing under the M6 before reaching Stretton Stop.

Stretton Stop, strategically located close to the railway and the Fosse Way, was once the location of a canal toll office. Part of a disused loop of the canal is still in water here, used for moorings and a boatyard. Leaving Stretton Stop behind, the canal takes a southerly course, through a cutting straight across the neck of the old Brinklow loop, before resuming a south-easterly direction towards Rugby. En route, the

Left *This ornate cast-iron bridge, built by the Britannia Foundry, Derby in 1837, marks the junction between the Oxford and Coventry Canals at Hawkesbury. To the right, the Oxford Canal passes through the Hawkesbury stop lock on its 77-mile journey to Oxford. Overlooking this tranquil scene on the outskirts of Coventry is the characterful Greyhound canalside pub.*

Above A narrow boat heads south near Easanhall Lane Bridge, Brinklow. This straight and steep-sided cutting, prone to landslips, vividly illustrates the techniques used to shorten the northern section of the Oxford Canal in the 1830s.

peacefully rural Oxford Canal passes through All Oaks Wood, across the neck of the Fennis Field loop, under the Crewe to Rugby railway line, before diving into the short Newbold Tunnel. The 250yd tunnel, cutting across the neck of another old loop, was constructed during the modernisation of the canal in the 1830s and was unusually built with two towpaths. One of the portals of the tunnel on the original course can still be seen to the south of Newbold Wharf and close to the village church. Newbold-on-Avon, now an unprepossessing suburb of Rugby, still possesses two canalside pubs – the Barley Mow and the Boat.

The original course of the Oxford Canal wound its way round the town of Rugby in a series of convoluted loops, but in the 1830s' modernisation these were abandoned – the new route crossing the valleys of the Rivers Swift and Avon on aqueducts and embankments. Short sections of the Rugby Wharf and Brownsover arms are still in water, used as moorings for leisure craft and a boatyard. Set close to the junction with the latter arm, the Bell & Barge is a conveniently located canalside pub. The industrialised surroundings of Rugby are soon left behind as the canal approaches the attractive canalside village of Hillmorton and the series of three paired locks – the first since leaving Hawkesbury Junction.

Hillmorton, overlooked by the wireless masts of Rugby Radio Station, is home to two boatyards, one of them being located along a short arm that was once part of the canal's pre-1830s course. To the south-west the electrified Euston to Crewe railway line parallels the canal for a short distance, parting company close to the Warwickshire/Northamptonshire border where the Old Royal Oak is a canalside pub conveniently located close to a boatyard. The course of the canal, cutting across the necks of old meandering loops, now passes under the M45 motorway and through gently rolling farmland where the evidence of medieval ridge and furrow strip farming can still be seen. For 1½ miles the trackbed of the ill-fated Great Central Railway, closed by Dr Beeching in 1966, closely parallels the canal as far as Navigation Bridge. Ahead lies Braunston Turn, and the junction with the Grand Union Canal.

Right The sylvan setting of the Oxford Canal at Newbold-on-Avon. Beyond this tranquil mooring is the southern portal of Newbold Tunnel, constructed during the modernisation of the canal in the 19th century.

Above Clifton Bridge and boatyard on the south-eastern outskirts of Rugby. *Just beyond the Clifton Cruisers boatyard is the short Clifton Arm, once part of the original meandering course of the Oxford Canal until the modernisation in the 1830s.*

Until 1805, Braunston was just yet another small village served by the meandering Oxford Canal. All this changed when the Grand Junction Canal to London was completed, sharing part of its route with the Oxford Canal between Braunston and Napton. During modernisation in the 1830s, the enormous loop of the Oxford Canal that meandered around the village was made completely redundant by the building of an aqueduct across the valley of the River Learn. Only a short section of this loop remains in water today to provide access to the large Braunston Marina with its associated boat yards, moorings and boat hire facilities. During its heyday, Braunston Junction was a bustling canal community, with boatbuilders, drydocks and transshipment warehouses. It was also the headquarters of Samuel Barlow Coal Company who were a major carrier of coal until as late as 1970. Their boats were noted for the elaborate hand painted decorations which were painstakingly carried out at the company's local boat yard. The large village of Braunston is set on a hill overlooking the junction and its churchyard contains the graves of many local boatmen who once plied their trade on the canal.

Leaving Braunston Turn in a south-westerly direction the joint course of the Oxford and Grand Union Canals crosses the River Learn on an 1830s aqueduct and out into remote, rolling countryside. It was this section of canal that kept the Oxford Canal Company profitable until the Second World War – extortionate toll charges were levied on cargoes being carried between London and Birmingham. Following a fairly straight course, the canal skirts the small village of Lower Shuckburgh until Napton Junction is reached. Here, the Grand Union branches off to the north on its wide-locked route to Warwick and Birmingham while the Oxford Canal follows its original contour-hugging course to the south.

Skirting the windmill and quarry on the western slopes of Napton Hill, the Oxford Canal passes the Napton Bridge Inn until the first of nine widely spaced Napton locks is reached. Close to the bottom lock and overlooked by the hillside village of Napton-on-the-Hill is the popular Folly canalside public house. Towards the top of this locked

Right Two graceful cast-iron bridges, built by the Horseley Ironworks in the 1830s, span the triangular junction and island between the Oxford and Grand Union Canals at Braunston Turn. The section of the canal between Braunston and Napton Junction kept the profits rolling in for the Oxford Canal Company who levied extortionate tolls on the Grand Union Canal until well into the 20th century.

section the Old Engine House Arm, now used for moorings, was once used by boats delivering coal to a steam pumping engine used to maintain water levels to the summit. Here, close to the small hamlet of Marston Doles, an old warehouse was once used as an office by British Waterways.

There now follows an 11-mile summit pound that winds its lonely and tortuous course around the contours, skirting 600ft Berry Hill before executing a near-180° turn around the base of Wormleighton Hill. This is a most delightful section of the Oxford Canal to travel along – either by boat or on foot – and the picturesque village of Wormleighton with its 13th century church and 16th century manor house is well worth the short detour. Passing Fenny Compton Wharf, the Wharf canalside pub and Fenny Marina the canal enters a deep and

Right *Man's best friend keeps an eye on his owner's narrowboat as it negotiates the top lock of the Napton flight of nine locks at Marston Dole.*

Right *The summit pound of the Oxford Canal executes a near 180° turn as it skirts the western slopes of Wormleighton Hill.*

narrow rock cutting. Still referred to as Fenny Tunnel, this cutting was once two tunnels which were opened up in 1870 to help relieve a notorious bottleneck. Closely parallelling the canal at this point is the former GWR route from London to Birmingham.

Emerging from the 'tunnel', the final section of the summit pound soon skirts Wormleighton Reservoir and a feeder from Boddington Reservoir – both built to help alleviate water shortages on this section. The Claydon flight of five locks, lowering the canal 30ft down towards Oxford, marks the end of the summit pound. Three further locks – Elkington's, Varney's and Broadmoor – are encountered on the journey down to the village of Cropredy where the old wharves, warehouses and toll offices are still intact. The Red Lion is a picturesque and popular pub conveniently situated close to the solitary Cropredy Lock. The

Left *Cropredy Wharf offers good moorings close to excellent shopping and refreshment facilities in the heart of this picturesque village.*

Left *Cropredy Lock seen through the arch of Bridge 152. Here, the River Cherwell flows in from the north east to accompany the Oxford Canal as far south as the village of Thrupp.*

Above Banbury Lock is located close to the centre of this bustling town. In the foreground is the first of the lifting bridges that are a feature of the Oxford Canal between here and Oxford.

River Cherwell now joins company as far as the outskirts of Oxford – its meandering course being closely followed, and in places being utilised, by the canal.

Three widely-spaced locks – Slat Mill, Bourton and Hardwick – take the Oxford Canal down to the town of Banbury. The outskirts of the town start at the latter lock where the busy M40 motorway is carried across the canal on a modern concrete structure. The next two miles are characterised by the spreading industrial estates, roads and housing estates that encroach down to the banks of the canal. Banbury Lock, located adjacent to the bus station and close to a boatyard, precedes the first of the pretty lifting bridges that characterise the route from here to Oxford.

South-east of Banbury, the Oxford Canal continues its idyllic, winding route along the valley of the River Cherwell, closely paralleled and criss-crossed by the GWR railway line to Oxford. At Grant's Lock even the M40 motorway joins company along this natural corridor for two miles. Oblivious of the more modern forms of transport, the canal serenely slides through the watermeadows, passing under numerous lifting bridges and through King's Sutton Lock. The picturesque village of King's Sutton, with its village green and beautiful spired church, lies on the hillside overlooking the valley but is not easily reached on foot from the canal.

Leaving King's Sutton behind, the Oxford Canal executes a sharp S-bend, passing under the M40 motorway, through Nell Bridge Lock and the curiously diamond-shaped Aynho Weir Lock. At the latter, the River Cherwell crosses on the level from the east to the west side of the canal and care needs to be taken by boat users to avoid the weir. One mile to the south is Aynho Wharf where the old warehouse is still intact and where there is a boatyard and moorings. Sandwiched between the canal and railway at this point is the popular and aptly named Great Western public house – needless to say, trains no longer stop at Aynho station!

South of Aynho Wharf, the Oxford Canal passes into Oxfordshire and soon encounters the 12ft-deep Somerton Deep Lock, one of the

Right Tranquil moorings at Aynho Wharf where the Great Western Arms is a conveniently located pub between Aynho Bridge and the nearby railway line.

Above *The neatly manicured setting of Allen's Lock on the outskirts of Upper Heyford. Peace and tranquility now reign in this lovely part of Oxfordshire since the closure of the nearby USAF base.*

deepest narrow locks in the country. Willow trees line the adjoining canal and river banks, making them indistinguishable from one another as they flow through the tranquil watermeadows of the Cherwell Valley. Next comes Heyford Common Lock, followed by Allen's Lock where a lane leads to the thatched, stone village of Upper Heyford. The canal and river follow a sweeping curve through woodland, past Heyford Mill to the neighbouring village of Lower Heyford where the wharf and old warehouse are now used by a boat hire company. Heyford Station, served by trains between Oxford and Banbury, is conveniently located for towpath walkers next to the wharf.

Continuing its southward meandering route along the beautiful Cherwell Valley, the Oxford Canal passes through a mixture of watermeadows and woodland, en route passing the grounds of 17th century Rousham Park and through Dashwood's, Northbrook and Pigeon's Locks. Old quarries, the site of an old cement works and the route of the Roman Akeman Street are all encountered on this idyllic section. The railway again crosses the canal near Enslow Bridge where the Rock of Gibraltar is a much-frequented canalside pub. Rounding a bend the canal encounters Baker's Lock, named after a former landlord of the pub, where the River Cherwell and canal merge for the next mile to Shipton Weir Lock. Rounding a further bend the Oxford Canal passes under the railway yet again, skirting the village of Shipton-on-Cherwell with its superbly located church before reaching Thrupp. This delightful canal village with its boatyard marks the point where the canal and River Cherwell part company. A delightful place to tie-up and take refreshments at the two canalside pubs – the Boat Inn and the Jolly Boatman. Soon the outskirts of Kidlington are reached at Langford Lane Bridge, where the Wise Alderman is yet another conveniently located canalside pub.

The Oxford Canal skirts the western edge of sprawling Kidlington, encountering Roundham Lock before passing under the railway for the umpteenth time. The village is left behind at Kidlington Green Lock and for the next two miles the canal passes through open countryside to Duke's Lock, where the railway draws in close from the west to join

Right *The boatyard and wharf at Lower Heyford, conveniently located for towpath walkers and boat users adjacent to Heyford Station on the Oxford to Banbury railway line.*

company for the last three miles to Oxford. Just beyond Duke's Lock is Duke's Cut, a ¼-mile channel with one lock that links the Oxford Canal with the River Thames. It was built in 1789 by the Duke of Marlborough and leased to the canal company in 1798.

On its final approach to Oxford the canal passes under several more of the attractive lifting bridges common to this southern section. Close to Wolvercote Lock the Plough is a popular canalside pub. As we near our destination, with the railway always present to the west, the gardens of Victorian houses and allotments can be seen running down to the canal banks. Moorings and boatyards precede the junction with Isis (or Louse) Lock, where a short cut carries the canal under the railway line to the River Thames. Beyond the junction with the cut, the canal continues for a further ¼-mile past Worcester College to its terminus close to Nuffield College.

Right Half hidden in a tranquil wooded setting, Shipton-on-Cherwell church overlooks an idyllic section of the Oxford Canal as it approaches the sprawling outskirts of Kidlington.

Right The secluded Pigeon's Lock is set in woodland close to a disused quarry, old cement works and the course of Roman Akeman Street.

REGENT'S CANAL

U NTIL THE OPENING of the Grand Junction Canal, canal traffic from Birmingham to London had to travel a circuitous route via the Oxford Canal, opened in 1790. Completion of the Grand Junction to the Paddington Basin in 1801 cut 60 miles off this journey. The canal terminus at Paddington was located at the western end of New Road (now Marylebone, Euston and Pentonville Roads), an 18th-century thoroughfare which, at that time, marked the northern edge of London. Goods then had to be transshipped from the canal boats to horsedrawn wagons for the final part of their journey to the City.

It was not long before plans were put forward for a canal to link Paddington with the City. By 1811 John Nash was involved in the design of nearby Regent's Park. After an initial scheme which included the new canal running through the centre of the park, the final route agreed upon took it along the northern boundary. The Royal Assent for the building of the Regent's Canal was passed by Parliament in July 1812. The final route commenced at Little Venice, where it formed a junction with the Paddington Arm of the Grand Junction, to a large ship basin at Limehouse where the canal was linked to the River Thames by a ship lock. The canal was to be 8½-miles in length and would incorporate two tunnels, at Maida Hill and Islington. Construction work started in October of that year with James Morgan as engineer and John Nash as one of the company's directors. Work continued over the next eight years and the full route between Paddington and Limehouse, built at a cost of just over £700,000, was officially opened in August 1820.

In addition to the important ship basin at Limehouse, the New Basin (or City Road Basin), located east of Islington Tunnel, became an important distribution point for London traders. One of the first companies to move here was Pickfords who transferred their depot from the Paddington basin. Other important basins located along the canal

Above *Modern architecture contrasts strongly with the former lock-keeper's cottage at Mile End Lock in east London.*

Left *Overlooked by a tree-lined avenue of elegant houses, moored canal boats make a colourful scene at Little Venice. Here, the Regent's Canal forms a junction with the Paddington Arm of the Grand Union Canal.*

Above *Modern housing development in an attractive canalside setting at Gunmaker's Arms Bridge – a peaceful counterpoint to the nearby busy Mile End Road.*

were at Cumberland Market, St Pancras, Battlebridge and Wenlock.

In 1830 the 1¼-mile Hertford Union Canal was built to link the Regent's Canal to the River Lee Navigation. This short canal, or cut, forms a junction close to Old Ford Lock and runs along the boundary of Victoria Park. Often referred to as 'Duckett's', it was built by Sir George Duckett and, following his bankruptcy, was purchased by the Regent's Canal Company in 1857.

With a drop in height of over 80ft between Little Venice and Limehouse, twelve locks were required along the length of the Regent's Canal. 56,000 gallons of water were required every time a lock was filled so water supply problems concentrated the minds of the engineers. To help overcome this, interconnecting paired locks were constructed throughout. Water was initially pumped from the Thames at Chelsea, via the Grand Junction Waterworks Company, but this soon proved to be too expensive. Backpumping water from the Thames at Limehouse was not an ideal solution either. Therefore, in 1835, the Regent's Canal Company built the Brent Reservoir, now located close to the North Circular Road, and water was supplied from the reservoir to the canal, via a feeder near Harlesden and the Paddington Arm of the Grand Junction Canal. The final solution to the water supply problem came about in 1929 when the Regent's Canal Company purchased the Grand Junction, thus forming what is now the Grand Union Canal.

During its first full year, 1821-1822, the Regent's Canal carried nearly 195,000 tons of goods, rising to nearly 625,000 tons by 1835, the bulk of which consisted of coal, bricks, timber, road and building materials. Industries soon sprang up along the canal and local trade was far heavier than through trade to other parts of the country. This increase in traffic soon caused delays for barges wishing to pass through Islington Tunnel. Due to the lack of a towpath barges had to be legged through the dank tunnel. The Company introduced a steam-powered tug service in 1826 and this helped to speed up transit times. However, due to the fumes given off by the tug this was eventually replaced by a chain-operated version which remained in service until the 1930s.

From the onset barges were hauled along the canal by horses but in

1925 petrol-driven tractors were introduced. This method of haulage soon proved to be a success as the tractors were able to haul two barges instead of one, with a 50% saving in time. However, horses still continued to be used until the mid 1950s.

The early success of the canal was soon tempered by the opening of the London & Birmingham Railway in 1837. This was soon followed by the Great Western Railway in 1838, the London & York Railway in 1852 and the Midland Railway in 1868. The London termini of these railway companies were all located along the New Road, in close proximity to the Regent's Canal. From west to the east along the New Road the railway termini were located at Paddington, Marylebone, Euston, St Pancras and King's Cross. As with canals throughout the country the Regent's Canal soon had to face stiff competition from the

Right *The latticework of two enormous gasometers overlook a grafitti-covered factory wall in Hackney where coal was once delivered by barge to the wharves of Gas, Light & Coke Company.*

railways. Two schemes were even drawn up in 1845 and 1883 to convert the canal into a railway but these never materialised. Over the following years traffic continued to decline and by the onset of World War I the canal was taken over by the Board of Trade. In 1929 the Regent's Canal was amalgamated with the Grand Junction Canal and other canals to form the Grand Union Canal. Nationalisation followed in 1948 and in 1963 control of the canal passed into the hands of the British Waterways Board. Although commercial traffic had virtually disappeared by the 1970s, the canal has become increasingly popular for leisure activities and its future is now assured.

A journey along the Regent's Canal

After years of neglect the Regent's Canal is now an attractive and fascinating waterway that offers many diverting opportunities for both the boat user and walker. Probably the best way to see the Regent's

Right This colourful scene at Little Venice is reminiscent of the canals in Amsterdam. These residential moorings and their well tended gardens are overlooked by tree-lined avenues of elegant houses in a tranquil part of west London.

Canal, its much-improved environment and wildlife, is to walk along the 8½-mile towpath.

Our journey to Limehouse starts at Little Venice, the junction between the Paddington Arm of the Grand Union Canal and the Regent's Canal and close to Warwick Avenue underground station. Once known as the Paddington Stop, Little Venice supposedly received its name from the poet Robert Browning who once lived nearby. Elegant Victorian houses and gardens overlook this attractive mooring, with its large number of colourful canal boats and former toll office. Canal boat cruises and a water bus operate from here to Camden. To the south-east the modern concrete flyover of the Westway crosses the entrance to the old Paddington Basin.

Flanked on either side by elegant houses the canal proceeds in a north-easterly direction until the entrance to the short Maida Hill Tunnel is reached. The 272yd tunnel burrows under the busy Edgware Road and has no towpath, thus barges had to be 'legged' through while the horse was taken over the top to rejoin the towpath close to Lisson Grove bridge. Beyond the bridge were once extensive moorings where goods were transshiped between barges and the Great Central Railway's Marylebone goods depot, now a modern housing estate. The towpath now passes under two bridges carrying the former Great Central Railway line from Marylebone and the Metropolitan Line from Baker Street. A short distance to the north-west is Lord's cricket ground, the surface of which was constructed from the soil removed during the construction of the Maida Hill Tunnel.

The Regent's Canal now enters a deep cutting before it skirts Regent's Park and London Zoo. The park was once Henry VIII's hunting forest and its present layout and surrounding terraces of Regency houses were designed by John Nash in the early 19th century. Several attractive cast-iron bridges cross the canal along this stretch. The most famous of these is Macclesfield Road Bridge, also known as Blow-up Bridge after a consignment of gunpowder ignited while being transported on a barge in 1874. Beyond the bridge, on the south bank, lie the 36 acres of London Zoo, designed by Decimus Burton in 1827. The modern aviary,

Above *A smart cafe looks down over the western portal of Maida Hill Tunnel where the Regent's Canal burrows under the busy Edgware Road. As no towpath was provided in the tunnel, boats had to be 'legged' through whilst the towing horses were led over the hill to the eastern end.*

Left A busy scene at Camden Lock, the first encountered since Little Venice. Camden Lock is now the only paired lock left intact on the Regent's Canal as all of the others have been singled by converting one of the chambers into a weir. Water buses regularly ply the canal between here and Little Venice with an intermediate stop at London Zoo. Beyond the lock, crowds of tourists throng the trendy Chalk Farm Road on their pilgrimage to nearby Camden Market.

designed by Lord Snowdon in 1965, is a prominent architectural feature located adjacent to the towpath. A canal waterbus connects the zoo with Camden and Little Venice.

Immediately beyond the zoo the Regent's Canal swings sharply to the north. At this point the truncated remains of the Cumberland Arm can be seen. Now used for boat moorings and a floating restaurant, the Arm once extended ¾-mile to serve Cumberland Market, situated close to Euston Station. The basin was filled in with rubble after World War II and in its place are now blocks of flats and allotments. Passing under Water Meeting Bridge and Grafton Bridge the canal then swings round in a leisurely curve to pass under the main railway line from Euston before reaching the site of Dingwall's Timber Wharf, Dock Basin and Hampstead Road Locks. The once-busy canalside warehouses and underground vaults are now used for a variety of purposes including television and radio studios, the famous Camden Lock Centre and a weekend market. A waterbus service operates from here to London Zoo and Little Venice.

Hampstead Road Top Lock, the first of twelve on the canal, is actually situated on Chalk Farm Road and features an early 19th century castellated former lock-keeper's cottage. The lock, with its original paddle gear, is now the only remaining double lock on the canal. The others were rebuilt in the 1970s with the second lock of each pair being converted into a weir. Two further locks, Hawley and Kentish Town, follow in quick succession. Reminders of the days when barges were horsedrawn are provided by the deep grooves worn into bridge structures along the canal. Protective iron guards, worn thin by the towing ropes, can still be seen under Camden Street Bridge.

The canal continues on its gently curving route, passing under the former Midland Railway line from St Pancras station, to St Pancras Lock. Immediately to the east of the railway bridge, constructed in 1868, lies the short St Pancras Basin. The site of a basin serving the Great Northern Railway coal wharves lies a short distance past the lock. The basin has now been filled in and the surrounding area is part of a major redevelopment scheme. A former coal depot on the opposite side

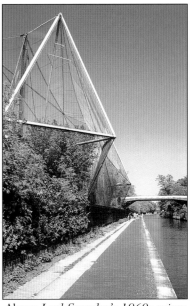

Above Lord Snowdon's 1960s aviary looms over the towpath as the Regent's Canal passes London Zoo. The zoo was opened in 1827 and houses one of the largest collections of wild animals in the world. A waterbus service along the canal links it with Camden Lock and Little Venice.

of the canal has now become the Camley Street Natural Park, its former derelict state being transformed into a habitat for wild life in the 1980s. Dominating the scene are the enormous cast-iron gas holders that were built by the Imperial Gas Company between 1861 and 1883 and the graceful curving roof of St Pancras Station. The canal soon passes over the twin Copenhagen Tunnels which carry the former Great Northern Railway's main line from King's Cross Station.

Maiden Lane Bridge, carrying York Way over the Regent's Canal, is soon followed by Battlebridge Basin. This large basin was built in 1825 by William Horsfall and is the site of Boadicea's battle with the occupying Romans in AD61. The basin is now overlooked by converted warehouses, the popular Waterside Inn and the London Canal Museum.

The museum was opened in March 1992 by the Princess Royal and

Right The former lock keeper's cottage at St Pancras Lock where one of the paired locks has been converted into a weir. Beyond the lock is the clubhouse of the St Pancras Cruising Club and moorings in St Pancras Basin. In the distance, the former Midland Railway line from St Pancras Station to Derby passes over the canal on a girder bridge.

is housed in a former warehouse built in the 1850s for Carlo Gatti, the famous ice cream manufacturer. Blocks of ice were imported from Norway and carried on the Regent's Canal from Limehouse Basin to Battlebridge Basin. Beneath the warehouse are two vast ice wells, one of which has been partially excavated and is on show to the public. The museum tells the story of the development of London's canals, from the early days as an important trade route, to today's more leisurely pursuits, and includes an exhibition on the history of London's Docklands, and a restored 1940s working tug boat. (London Canal Museum, 12-13 New Wharf Road, King's Cross, London N1 9RT. Tel. 0171 713 0836. Open Tuesday to Sunday and Bank Holidays except Christmas and New Year). Leaving Battlebridge Basin the canal approaches Islington Tunnel, passing en route the Regent's Wharf office complex, converted warehouses and the award-winning Barnsbury Estate.

Left *A sylvan scene at the eastern portal of Islington Tunnel. As with Maida Hill Tunnel, no towpath was provided and boats had to be 'legged' through whilst the towing horses were led over the hill and through the busy streets of Islington to rejoin the canal at the far portal. In the 19th century a steam tug was introduced to speed up transit through the tunnel. This was later replaced by a chain-operated version which remained in service until the 1930s.*

Above *A narrowboat waits to pass through Sturts Lock. On the wall of a large building near the lock can still be seen the name of Gainsborough Pictures. Many famous British films were made in these studios, including 'Oh, Mr Porter' and 'The Lady Vanishes'.*

As with Maida Hill Tunnel, the 960yd Islington Tunnel has no towpath and, until 1826, barges had to be 'legged' through. In that year the Company introduced a steam-powered tug service but, due to the fumes given off by the tug this was eventually replaced by a chain-operated version which remained in service until the 1930s. In horse-drawn days the horse was led over the top of the tunnel to rejoin the canal at the eastern portal. Towpath walkers also have to take to the streets, passing the Half Moon Crescent Housing Cooperative Estate, the Royal Agricultural Hall and Camden Passage.

Rejoining the canalside walk at the eastern end of the tunnel the walker soon reaches City Road Lock, an attractive lock-keeper's cottage and the large City Road Basin. The four acre basin was once a hive of industry and contained wharfs operated by Fellows, Morton & Clayton and Pickfords along with handling facilities for timber and grain. Recent development schemes have reduced the size of the basin and the former warehouses have now been replaced by modern structures. Between this basin and the nearby Wenlock Basin can be found the popular Narrowboat canalside pub.

Wenlock Basin, built in 1826 and named after the Wenlock Iron Company, is much smaller and is now used as moorings for leisure craft. Following the canalside walk Sturts Lock is soon reached where a large canalside building was once the headquarters of Gainsborough Pictures It was in these studios that many famous British films, including 'Oh, Mr. Porter' and 'The Lady Vanishes', were made between 1922 and 1950. Further along, the towpath passes the entrance to Kingsland Basin, built in 1830 for handling stone and timber and now used as a mooring for leisure craft. The canal passes through Haggerston, the in-filled Haggerston Basin and several housing estates, until Actons Lock, once the site of a busy timber wharf, is reached.

Entering Bethnall Green, the towpath passes under Cat & Mutton Bridge, once the site of a canalside pub, passing a converted warehouse and several large gas holders. Coal for the gasworks was once delivered to a wharf by barge. Beyond here the former Great Eastern Railway line from Liverpool Street station to Cambridge crosses the canal, followed immediately by Mare Street Bridge. A small timber wharf and basin were once located between these two bridges. The route of the canal now follows a sweeping curve, temporarily leaving behind the industrial landscape as it skirts the south-western edge of Victoria Park, London's oldest municipal park. The park, extending to over 200 acres, was laid out in 1845 by James Pennthorne, a protegé of John Nash. The towpath passes under elegant Bonner Hall Bridge, providing access to the park, before reaching Old Ford Lock and the popular Royal Cricketers canalside pub.

A short distance south-east of the lock is the junction with the Hertford Union Canal. The 1¼-mile canal, skirting the south-eastern boundary of Victoria Park, was built in 1830 to link the Regent's Canal to the River Lee Navigation. Often referred to as 'Duckett's', it was built by Sir George Duckett and, following his bankruptcy, was purchased by the Regent's Canal Company in 1857.

The Regent's Canal continues in a southerly direction, passing several former warehouses, former railway-connected wharves and under the Liverpool Street to Norwich railway line. The next lock to be reached is Mile End Lock with adjoining lock-keeper's cottage, warehouse and the New Globe public house. The canal then passes under Gunmaker's Arms Bridge, skirting attractive canalside residences, to Johnson's Lock where the old paddle gear has now been restored. The final stretch of the canal, once heavily industrialised, continues to Salmon Lane Lock and under Commercial Road Bridge to the twelfth lock, Commercial Road Lock.

Limehouse Basin, previously known as Regent's Canal Dock, is entered beneath an attractive 19th century railway viaduct. The large ship basin, covering 11 acres and connected to the River Thames by a ship lock, was once a busy transshipment centre where sea-going vessels of up to 3000 tons offloaded their cargoes onto canal barges for their journey inland. Limehouse Basin is also linked to the River Lee Navigation via the Limehouse Cut. This was built across the Isle of Dogs in 1770, 50 years before the construction of the Regent's Canal, to provide improved access for boats from the Thames to the River Lee.

Above *Tower blocks and grafitti dominate this peaceful scene of young fishermen at Commercial Road Lock. The twelfth and final lock on the Regent's Canal and 80ft lower than Camden Lock, it is located at the northern end of Limehouse Basin.*

Commercial traffic into the basin ceased in 1970 and since then the area has been the subject of a major development scheme providing a marina, shops, offices, public houses and restaurants. The Barley Mow, formerly the harbour master's office, is a popular public house located at the entrance to the dock and Limehouse Station is served by the recently opened Docklands Light Railway.

Right Upmarket housing development has now replaced the bustling warehouses and wharves around Limehouse Basin. Here, the Regent's Canal is connected to the River Thames by the modern Limehouse Ship Lock.

Right Old and new at Limehouse. Floating gin palaces rub shoulders with canal narrowboats in Limehouse Basin. In the distance a Docklands Light Railway train rattles across the graceful brick viaduct built in 1838 for the London & Blackwall Railway.

STRATFORD-UPON-AVON CANAL

T HE 42 MILES of the River Avon from Tewkesbury, where it flows into the River Severn, to Stratford-upon-Avon was first made navigable in the early 17th century. With its link by pack horse route to the Midlands and navigable river links, via the Avon and Severn, to Gloucester and Bristol, the town soon became an important transshipment centre for cross-country trade. However, the building of canals in the 18th century took trade away from the town and local businessmen were soon pressing for a canal that linked Stratford to the burgeoning network of the Midlands. Several different proposals were put forward in the latter part of that century, the final one chosen being a route for a narrow canal from the newly authorised Worcester & Birmingham Canal at King's Norton, hence giving it a direct route into Birmingham, to a terminus in Stratford. The line of the new canal would also take it very close to the newly-constructed Warwick & Birmingham Canal at Lapworth where a short link would be constructed, hence giving it access via the Grand Junction Canal to London. To appease the Worcester & Birmingham Canal the terminus at Stratford was not designed to link with the River Avon, a matter which was subsequently changed by an Act of Parliament in 1815.

The Act of Parliament for the building of the Stratford-upon-Avon Canal was passed in March 1793, authorising a capital of £120,000 with the power to raise another £60,000 if necessary. Josiah Clowes was appointed Chief Engineer and work commenced from King's Norton Junction in November of the same year. By the middle of 1796 the first 9¾ miles had been built, but by then all of the capital had been used. Construction work ground to a halt, only recommencing three years later when extra capital was raised by a further Act of Parliament. In the meantime Josiah Clowes had died and his assistant, Samuel Potter, was

Above *Designed to allow the towing lines of horse-drawn boats to pass through without interruption, these attractive split bridges are unique to the Stratford-upon-Avon Canal. This one overlooks the restored canal buildings at Kingswood Junction.*

Above The restored western portal of Brandwood Tunnel features the canal company seal – a bust of William Shakespeare. The 352yd tunnel, the only one on the canal, is set in a leafy but litter-strewn cutting in the south-eastern suburbs of Birmingham.

appointed in his place. By 1802, construction work had extended the canal as far as Kingswood Junction and the short link with the Warwick & Birmingham Canal. The northern section of the canal was now complete and commercial trade, especially the carrying of coal from the Midlands, brought much-needed revenue to the company.

However, work on the southern section from Kingswood to Stratford did not commence until 1812 after further funding had to be sought. By 1813, the canal had been extended to a large basin at Wootton Wawen which remained the southern terminus for the next three years. A further Act of Parliament was passed in 1815 to allow the canal to be linked with the River Avon at Stratford and the canal, 25½ miles in length with 54 locks, four aqueducts and one tunnel, was opened throughout in June 1816 at a total cost of nearly £300,000.

Trade on the new canal was initially brisk with coal being carried from the Midlands via the newly-opened Dudley No. 2 and the Worcester & Birmingham Canals. In its heyday 50,000 tons of coal, representing over 25% of all trade on the canal, were carried annually down to Stratford. Other important cargoes included salt, corn and limestone. The opening of the horse-drawn Stratford & Moreton Tramway in 1826 helped to boost trade even further. However, the expected through trade between Birmingham and the River Severn never materialised as the neighbouring Worcester & Birmingham Canal provided a more direct route. The situation was not improved when, in 1830, the W&B leased the lower part of the River Avon between Tewkesbury and Evesham thus effectively blocking the Stratford-upon-Avon Canal's direct access to the Severn.

As with other canals during this period the coming of the railways soon sounded their death knell. Tolls were reduced in a vain attempt to remain competitive following the opening of the London & Birmingham Railway in 1838 and, in the face of ever-increasing competition, the Stratford-upon-Avon Canal was taken over by the Oxford, Worcester & Wolverhampton Railway in 1845. Trade on the canal inevitably declined and with the opening of the Stratford-upon-Avon Railway in 1860 the situation worsened further. In 1863 the railway-owners of the canal were themselves taken over by the Great Western Railway and by the end of the 19th century the canal, with very little commercial trade, was in a sorry state of repair. Somehow or other the weed-choked canal struggled on until the 1930s when the southern section from Kingswood to Stratford had become completely derelict. The northern section saw very little traffic and was in a poor state of repair when the canal was nationalised in 1948. Complete abandonment of the canal was sought in 1958 but this action was stopped by the timely intervention of the Stratford-upon-Avon Canal Society and the Inland Waterways Association. The closure plan was rescinded in 1959 and a year later the National Trust took over the 13-mile southern section between Kingswood Junction and Stratford. With Government grants, financial assistance from the National Trust and a

Left *Edstone Aqueduct carries the canal on 14 brick arches across a road, river and railway close to the village of Bearley. The canal, set in a cast-iron trough, runs at a higher level than the towpath – a feature unique to the aqueducts on this canal.*

vast army of unpaid volunteer workers, assisted by Army personnel and even prisoners, this section was fully restored and reopened in 1964. The southern section of the canal, the first in the country to be restored by volunteer labour, was eventually handed back to British Waterways in 1988, thus eliminating the need for boat users to purchase a National Trust licence. Since restoration, the Stratford-upon-Avon Canal has been increasingly popular for pleasure boats completing the Avon Ring circuit via the Rivers Avon and Severn and the Worcester & Birmingham Canal.

A journey along the Stratford-upon-Avon Canal
King's Norton is where the Stratford-upon-Avon Canal forms a junction with the Worcester & Birmingham Canal, five miles from Gas Street Basin in the heart of the city. This important connection and, until

Right *The guillotine stop lock at Kings Norton, close to the canal's junction with the Worcester & Birmingham Canal. Now disused, this unusual piece of equipment was installed to to prevent water flowing from the Stratford-upon-Avon Canal to the W&B.*

1917, the link with the Midlands coalfields via the now-closed Dudley No. 2 Canal, brought about much of the canal's early prosperity. When the Stratford-upon-Avon Canal was built, a stop lock was installed at King's Norton to prevent the water supply flowing from the canal to the neighbouring Worcester & Birmingham. This unusual stop lock, located a short distance from the actual junction and now disused, has two wooden guillotine gates that once operated vertically within a steel frame. For the first five miles the canal wends its way through the south eastern leafy suburbs of Birmingham, first passing under the Lifford Lane swing bridge before burrowing through the attractively restored portal of Brandwood Tunnel. This 352yd tunnel, the only one on the canal and its western portal proudly displaying a stone plaque of William Shakespeare, has no towpath and walkers must follow the recently restored horse path over the hill.

Emerging from the wooded cutting to the east of the tunnel, the canal and its newly-resurfaced towpath soon reach Bridge 3 with its attendant boatyard, moorings and the Horse Shoe canalside pub. Still hidden from its surrounding suburban landscape by tree-lined cuttings, the canal now executes several sharp turns to take a south-easterly direction through Warstock and Yardley Green, crossing the little River Cole on Cole Aqueduct near the suburb of Shirley. Here, there is an electrically-operated lift bridge and the appropriately-named Drawbridge public house. Shirley Station, located on the Birmingham to Stratford-upon-Avon railway line, is but a short distance to the north of the bridge.

South-east of Shirley Bridge the canal passes under the railway line with access to Whitlocks End Halt from Bridge 9. Now entering pleasant countryside, the Stratford-upon-Avon Canal continues its winding route through wooded cuttings, occasionally passing under the attractive brick-arched bridges that are typical of this northern section. At Bridge 16 a feeder maintains levels in the canal with water from the nearby Earlswood Reservoirs. Water from the three separate reservoirs, covering an area of 85 acres, was once pumped to the canal by a steam engine until the 1930s. Located close to the junction with the feeder are moorings, boatyard and the headquarters of the Earlswood Motor Yacht

Above *The Stratford-upon-Avon Canal passes secretly through the south eastern suburbs of Birmingham hidden away from view in deep, wooded cuttings.*

Above Kingswood Junction, where a short cut links the canal to the Grand Union, is a mecca for canal enthusiasts. The former canal buildings have been sympathetically restored and are now used as offices and stores by British Waterways. A car park and picnic area have been provided in a wooded setting overlooking the canal.

Club. One mile further along the canal, at Waring's Green, are further moorings, boat yard and the Blue Bell canalside pub. Continuing on its leisurely tree-lined rural route, the canal passes under the busy M42 motorway before reaching Hockley Heath. Here, there is a small arm, formerly a coal wharf, with a boatyard, moorings and the Wharf Tavern canalside pub. The northern section of the canal then passes under two more lift bridges as it approaches the first of the Lapworth flight of locks.

A total of 19 locks take the canal, accompanied by a well-surfaced towpath, a distance of one-and-a-half miles down to Kingswood Junction and the short link to the Grand Union Canal. Several cast-iron split bridges, unique to the Stratford-upon-Avon Canal, cross the canal at various points along the flight. These bridges have a narrow gap running through their centre which allowed the towing lines of horse-drawn boats to pass through. At Bridge 31, between Locks 5 and 6, a road leads to National Trust-owned Packwood House. This delightful 16th century timber-framed country house, famous for its yew topiary, is open to the public. (Telephone 01564 782024 for details of opening times.) Accompanied by pretty lock keeper's cottages, the Lapworth flight of locks are initially widely spaced out, but from Lock 6 to Lock 14 they are grouped dramatically close together. Near Lock 14 is the popular canalside Boot Inn.

Lock 19 takes the canal down to Kingswood Junction, a mecca for canal enthusiasts. A further lock takes the short junction canal down to the main line of the former Warwick & Birmingham Canal, now the Grand Union Canal. Bisecting the two canals at this important canal junction is the Birmingham to Warwick Railway line with Lapworth Station being conveniently located a short distance to the north.

The beautifully restored southern section of the Stratford-upon-Avon Canal commences at Lock 21, close to the short link with the Grand Union. One of the barrel-roofed lock-keeper's cottages, unique to the canal, is located opposite the small British Waterways maintenance workshop, once used by the National Trust during their guardianship of the southern section. During the period of restoration, a total of 36

Right Looking up the closely spaced Lapworth flight of locks from Lock 14. A small canal shop and the picturesque Boot Inn are conveniently located close to the flight.

Above Wootton Wawen Aqueduct, *built in 1813, carries the canal over the busy A34 road and has survived several collisions from lorries. Immediately beyond the aqueduct is a basin providing moorings and a boatyard. The scene is overlooked by the aptly-named Navigation Inn.*

locks were rebuilt between Kingswood Junction and Stratford. Continuing in a southerly direction through the remnants of the Forest of Arden, the canal passes through seven of these locks, interspersed by more of the unique split bridges and barrel-roofed lock-keeper's cottages, until the ugly modern structure of the M40 motorway bridge looms into view. With the continuous hum of traffic fading into the distance, four more widely spaced locks take the canal through delightful countryside to the hamlet of Lowsonford. A short distance before the hamlet is reached are the remains of a former railway bridge that once carried a branch line over the canal to Henley-in-Arden. In the hamlet, refreshments can be taken at the 14th century Fleur-de-Lys canalside pub.

From Lowsonford three more locks carry the canal to Yarningale Aqueduct where the well-restored towpath changes from the south to the north bank. The original iron structure was destroyed in a flood in July 1934 but quickly replaced by the present aqueduct one month later. The canal is carried in a cast-iron trough with the towpath at the side set below the level of the water. Set in the peaceful Warwickshire countryside the canal passes through five more widely spaced locks, the towpath changing sides several times, to arrive at Preston Bagot. This small, picturesque village contains several fine houses, 16th century manor house and the Crab Mill Inn.

There now begins a long pound with only one lock located in the 5½ miles between Preston Bagot and the Wilmcote flight of locks. From Preston Bagot the canal winds its rural route along the hillside above the valley of the River Alne. After two miles, the picturesque village of Wootton Wawen is reached. The basin, now providing moorings and a boatyard and awarded a Civic Trust award in 1972, was the temporary southern terminus of the canal between 1813 and 1816. The Navigation Inn is a popular canalside pub overlooking the basin. Within the village, designated a conservation area, are attractive half-timbered houses, 17th century manor house and the magnificent Church of St Peter, the oldest church in Warwickshire. Wootton Wawen railway station is located to the west of the village and is served by trains from Birmingham and Stratford. Immediately south west of the basin, the canal is carried over the busy A34 trunk road on a cast-iron aqueduct, built in 1813 and still surviving despite being hit several times by lorries.

Soon after the aqueduct the canal takes a south-easterly direction and after one and a half miles reaches the aptly-named Odd Lock, located to the north of the impressive Edstone Aqueduct. This cast-iron structure, again with a sunken towpath, carries the canal on 14 brick arches for 750ft across a river, railway line and road. Bearley railway station and the Golden Cross public house, half a mile to the east, can be easily reached on foot from the southern end of the aqueduct. Returning to its southerly and contour-hugging route the Stratford-

Left *Peaceful moorings opposite the Fleur-de-Lys public house at Lowsonford.*

Above *The attractively restored canal basin at Stratford-upon-Avon is connected to the River Avon by a wide-beam lock. The basin was once lined by wharves and warehouses and since restoration in the 1960s is a pleasantly landscaped stretch of water located close to the world famous Royal Shakespeare Theatre*

upon-Avon Canal is joined from the east by the Birmingham to Stratford railway line which closely parallels its route all the way to Stratford. Just before the village of Wilmcote, a row of cottages and winding hole mark the site of a stone wharf that was a busy transshipment centre in the mid-19th century. Limestone was carried by horse-drawn tramway from quarries to the wharf where it was loaded on to canal boats. A short distance to the south is the wharf and small, picturesque village of Wilmcote. Within the village is Mary Arden's Cottage, the home of Shakespeare's mother, a pub, hotel and attractive 19th century church. Pretty little Wilmcote Station, served by trains on the Birmingham to Stratford-upon-Avon railway line, is conveniently located a short distance to the east of Bridge 59. The planned replacement of this bridge by a fixed structure nearly brought about the abandonment of the canal by Warwickshire County Council in 1958. The threat, which would have effectively blocked the canal, triggered the eventual restoration of the then derelict southern section.

Half a mile to the south of Bridge 59, the Wilmcote flight of 11 locks drops the canal down towards Stratford, paralleled closely by the railway line and a well-maintained towpath. A further five locks take the canal secretively down through the semi-industrial outskirts of Stratford before emerging into an attractively restored basin. This flower-lined area of water, linked to the River Avon by a final wide-beam lock, was in the 19th century a busy transshipment centre with wharves and warehouses. All these have long gone, the formerly derelict site restored to its present state in the early 1960s, being replaced by moorings for numerous canal and river pleasure craft. The famous town of Stratford-upon-Avon needs no introduction to the reader, suffice to say that its streets are usually packed with tourists visiting the birthplace and home of William Shakespeare, his tomb in the 15th century Holy Trinity Church, the Royal Shakespeare Theatre and nearby Anne Hathaway's Cottage. Although restoration of the canal was completed by the National Trust in 1964, the Stratford-upon-Avon Canal Society still organise work parties of volunteers for towpath improvement work and scrub clearance.

Right *The canal version of 'Stop Me and Buy One' at Stratford-upon-Avon canal basin.*

Worcester & Birmingham Canal

Above *Passing through the flight of 30 locks at Tardebigge is slow progress and hard work.*

T HE WORCESTER & BIRMINGHAM CANAL was born at the height of Canal Mania towards the end of the 18th-century. Britain was then in the grip of the Industrial Revolution and the only route that canal traffic could take from Bristol, Gloucester and Worcester to the centre of Birmingham was via the River Severn, with its treacherous currents and shoals, to Stourport thence the Staffordshire & Worcestershire Canal to Aldersley and finally the Birmingham Canal. The Staffordshire & Worcestershire, engineered by James Brindley and opened in 1772, was a considerable financial success but this slow and roundabout route caused many delays and obviously added to the cost of transporting raw materials and goods.

In 1790 a proposal was put forward for a canal to link the River Severn at Worcester, thus cutting out the dangerous river navigation between that city and Stourport, to the centre of Birmingham. The promotors of this scheme, quite correctly, indicated that their canal was 30 miles shorter than the alternative routes. This one fact had the desired effect on financial backers and industrialists with the obvious savings in time and tolls. A Bill for the building of the Worcester & Birmingham Canal was put before Parliament in the same year but was defeated after much lobbying by the owners of the Birmingham and Staffordshire & Worcestershire Canals. The promoters of the new canal now sought, and gained, more active support from the industrialists of Birmingham who, quite naturally, would benefit from the opening of this much shorter route. A second Bill was put before Parliament in

1791 and this time it was successful. However, there were serious strings attached to the Bill that enabled the canal to be built.

It must also be noted that by 1792 the alternative route via the River Severn at Stourport to the centre of Birmingham had been reduced by 15 miles when the Stourbridge and Dudley Canals were opened. To appease the rival canal companies the Worcester & Birmingham had to agree to several financial guarantees to cover their loss of revenue and to erect a 7ft barrier between itself and the Birmingham Canal at Gas Street Basin. This infamous barrier, known as the Worcester Bar, was ostensibly erected to stop water loss between the two canals but in reality brought about a time-wasting and costly transshipment of cargoes.

The Worcester & Birmingham was originally designed as a wide canal but was eventually built with a combination of narrow locks and wide tunnels and bridges. This change of plan was not only due to

Right *Attractively restored lock-keeper's cottages at Blockhouse Lock in Worcester. Although located in the heart of this busy city, the well maintained canal towpath provides a peaceful alternative route for pedestrians and cyclists.*

rising costs and water supply problems, but also because the other linking canals, such as the Stratford-upon-Avon Canal, were of the narrow type. If the original plan had been followed then broad beam barges would have been able to travel all the way from Sharpness and Gloucester, via the River Severn, right into the centre of Birmingham without the need for transshipment of cargoes.

Thomas Cartwright was appointed Chief Engineer for the canal and by the autumn of 1795 the first three miles between Worcester Bar and Selly Oak had been completed. Work was also progressing on the notorious 2726yd King's Norton Tunnel and the construction of Upper and Lower Bittell Reservoirs. The latter had to be built to provide an adequate water supply to the summit of the canal, thus preventing the loss of water to neighbouring mill streams. By the end of that year serious financial problems were looming. Of the £180,000 estimated for the cost for constructing the whole canal, over £150,000 had

Left *The Boat and Railway pub is sandwiched between the Worcester & Birmingham Canal and the Birmingham to Bristol railway line at Stoke Works. Once the largest salt works in the world, Stoke Works was responsible for much of the canal's commercial traffic until the opening of the railway.*

Left The Worcester & Birmingham is one of the most heavily locked canals in the country. The flight of six locks at Offerton are easy work compared to that which lies ahead at Tardebigge.

already been spent and so an additional £70,000 had to be raised. However, work continued and by March 1797 boats could travel from Worcester Bar through King's Norton Tunnel to Hopwood Wharf, a distance of just over 8 miles. Due to continuing financial difficulties this remained the southern terminus of the canal until 1807 when the canal was completed as far as Tardebigge Old Wharf, just short of the planned Tardebigge Tunnel and the 217ft drop down to Stoke Prior.

A further Act of Parliament was passed in 1808 enabling the Worcester & Birmingham Canal Company to raise nearly an additional £170,000 to complete the canal to Worcester. To take the canal down from Tardebigge to Stoke Priors it was planned to build a total of 76 locks. However, there were concerns voiced that this large number of locks would not only create a major water supply problem but also add considerably to the length of time for a boat to transit. Following the completion of Tardebigge Tunnel in 1810 the new Chief Engineer, John

Left Slow progress up the Tardebigge flight of 30 locks. Small cottages are tucked in at intervals along the rural route of the canal as it wends its way through the Worcestershire hills.

Woodhouse, had installed a boat lift in place of the top lock. Although this seemed to work perfectly well during testing the canal company, acting on the advice of John Rennie, decided to opt for a reduced number of locks, totalling 36, to take the canal down to Stoke Priors.

Construction work on the Tardebigge flight of locks and adjacent reservoir started in 1812 and by 1815 the canal had reached Diglis Basin in Worcester. The Worcester & Birmingham Canal, its 30-mile length involving the construction of 58 locks, five tunnels and ten reservoirs, was officially opened on 4 December 1815, 24 years after the first Act of Parliament was passed and at an eventual cost of over three times the original estimate. In the same year the Worcester Bar in Birmingham was replaced by a stop lock.

For the first 26 years of its life the canal carried increasing quantities of industrial goods, raw coal, timber, grain and rock salt. Diglis and Lowesmoor were busy transshipment basins at Worcester which handled large amounts of traffic between the River Severn and the canal. To further extend its route, in 1825 the company leased the Lower River Avon from Tewkesbury to Evesham and in 1830 commenced carrying large quantities of rock salt from Stoke Works. But the initial success of the canal, albeit with large sums of money still owed for its construction, was shortlived. In 1841 the Birmingham & Gloucester Railway was opened and this had an immediate downward effect on the canal company's trade.

The Worcester & Birmingham hit back by reducing tolls and in 1852, after losing most of the Stoke Works salt trade to the railway, opened the Droitwich Canal. This short branch, designed to retrieve the salt carrying trade, connected the Droitwich Barge Canal with the main line of the Worcester & Birmingham at Hanbury Wharf. All of this was to no avail and soon the company was discussing the option of leasing the canal to the Oxford, Worcester & Wolverhampton Railway, a move which was eventually deemed illegal. Other plans that came to nothing included converting the whole canal to a railway. By the late 1860s, when no dividends to shareholders were being paid and the company still owed a large amount of money, the receivers were called

Right *Diglis Basin at the southern end of the Worcester & Birmingham Canal. To the right of the canal company's building are the two wide beam locks that link the canal with the fast-flowing River Severn.*

in. Eventually the canal was taken over in 1874 by the Sharpness New Docks Company with the new company being called the Sharpness New Docks & Gloucester & Birmingham Navigation Company.

After a few years the new company also started to lose money and without the profits from the Gloucester & Sharpness Canal the Worcester & Birmingham would have closed for good. Commercial traffic continued to decline during the early 20th century, the long-disused Droitwich arm was abandoned just prior to World War II, and despite nationalisation in 1948 trade had dwindled to traffic between two of Cadbury's factories at Bourneville and Blackpole and to Frampton-on-Severn on the Gloucester & Sharpness Canal. Even this had ceased by 1964. Following nationalisation, attempts were made to officially close the Worcester & Birmingham but this was averted by an increase in use by leisure boats and today the picturesque canal, a haven for wildlife, is an important link in the Midlands circuit.

Right Lowesmoor Wharf and basin, once a busy transshipment point, now provide extensive moorings for leisure boats in Worcester.

A journey along the Worcester & Birmingham Canal

We start our journey at Gas Street Basin in the heart of Birmingham, once surrounded by dank and decaying warehouses but now a shiny example to late 20th century optimism. A permanently open stop lock marks the start of the canal and the site of the famous Worcester Bar, a 7ft physical obstruction that, until 1815, separated the Worcester & Birmingham from the rest of the Birmingham canal network. Leaving the city centre basin the canal executes a 90° turn and is soon accompanied, at least as far as Bourneville, by its former arch enemy – the former Midland Railway route from Birmingham to Bristol. The surprisingly secluded course of the canal for the next five miles runs through the southern suburbs of the city, passing through the short Edgbaston Tunnel (the only one with a towpath) to Birmingham University before reaching the former junction with the Dudley No. 2 Canal. Completed in 1798 this canal was, until 1917, a through route to the Dudley No.1 Canal at Park Head Junction and the Netherton Branch of the Birmingham Canal. However, in that year, the 3795yds. long Lappal Tunnel (the fourth longest and one of the narrowest in Britain) collapsed and was never rebuilt.

Still following its suburban route and accompanied by the railway, the Worcester & Birmingham soon passes Selly Oak, Bournbrook and the Cadbury's Chocolate factory at Bourneville. The factory, opened in 1879, once generated a considerable amount of canal-borne trade which lasted until the 1960s. Close to Bridge 77 is the large garden village of Bourneville, built by the Quaker owners of the factory for their workers, and the recently-opened Cadbury World which tells the story of chocolate and its links with Victorian Birmingham. A further mile south is King's Norton Junction where the Worcester & Birmingham links with the northern end of the picturesque Stratford-upon-Avon Canal.

The two canals were once separated by a guillotine gate stop lock, installed to prevent the water supply flowing from one company's canal to the other. This unusual stop lock, now disused, has two wooden guillotine gates that operated vertically within a steel frame. The

Stratford-on-Avon Canal was built in two sections. The northern section, from King's Norton to Lapworth, opened in 1802, and the southern, from Lapworth to Stratford, opened in 1818. Commercial traffic, especially coal from the West Midlands' collieries, was initially heavy but competition was soon encountered with the opening of railways in the 1830s. By 1856 the canal had been bought by the Great Western Railway and by the end of the 19th century commercial traffic had declined substantially. Soon after the end of World War II the southern section was impassable and the northern section saw very little traffic. By 1955 closure was on the cards but with massive support from the public and the Inland Waterways Association this decision was rescinded and in 1960 the National Trust took over the southern section, completely restoring it by 1964. It thus became the first canal in Britain to be restored by voluntary labour. The southern section was eventually handed back to the British Waterways Board in 1988 and

Right The southern portal of Kings Norton Tunnel. This 2726yd tunnel, also known as Wast Hill Tunnel, was built to accommodate wide beam boats. During the 1870s a steam-powered tug service was introduced to speed up journey times and relieve congestion by towing several boats through in a 'train'. The towing animal, either horse or donkey, was led over the hill to rejoin its boat at the other end.

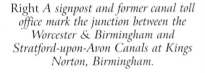

Right A signpost and former canal toll office mark the junction between the Worcester & Birmingham and Stratford-upon-Avon Canals at Kings Norton, Birmingham.

the canal, attractively rural throughout its length, now sees much activity from pleasure cruising.

A short distance from King's Norton Junction a feeder flows in from Wychall Reservoir to the west before the Worcester & Birmingham Canal enters a deep cutting on the approach to King's Norton Tunnel. Completed in 1797 the dank and dripping tunnel, with no towpath, is one of the longest still in use in Britain. Although the canal was eventually constructed for narrow boats, the tunnel was built to accommodate wide boats and thus there is room for two such boats to pass. However, due to the lack of towpath, horse drawn boats had to be 'legged' through until a steam-powered tug was introduced in the 1870s. This tug service speeded up journey times considerably and during busy periods helped to relieve congestion by towing several boats through in a 'train'. Meanwhile, the towing animal had to be led over the hill to rejoin the canal and its boat at the rural southern portal. It is

Right The Green Woodpecker *passes the Crown pub near Alvechurch on its leisurely journey towards Birmingham.*

interesting to note that at one time pairs of donkeys were preferred to horses for towing boats on the Worcester & Birmingham Canal.

Emerging from the tunnel mouth, the canal passes through a deep cutting before entering open country. The small settlement of Hopwood, the temporary southern terminus of the canal from 1797 to 1807, is but a short distance from the tunnel. For present day canal users, Hopwood contains moorings, a boat yard and the popular Hopwood House canalside pub. To the west lie the Lickey Hills and the large Upper Bittell Reservoir, built as a water supply for the summit of the canal. The reservoir is linked to Lower Bittell Reservoir and thence via a feeder to the canal, joining it one mile south-west of Hopwood. The lower reservoir, set in a wooded valley, does not feed the canal, being built to supplement water supplies to mills in the late 18th century. The canal now follows a picturesque contour-hugging route through the Worcestershire hills to the west of Alvechurch, passing

Left *The daffodils are in full bloom at these peaceful moorings in Alvechurch.*

under the M42 motorway just north of the village and then the Redditch to Litchfield railway line. Alvechurch Wharf provides a boatyard, moorings, shops and the attractive canalside Crown public house.

From Alvechurch the summit level of the canal wends its delightfully rural route along the side of a wooded valley before plunging into the 613yd Shortwood Tunnel. During the latter part of the 19th century canal boats were hauled through the tunnel by steam tugs. As with other W&B tunnels, Shortwood does not possess a towpath and walkers can follow the route once taken over the hill by towing donkeys and horses. Half a mile to the south of the tunnel the canal passes through a landscape of fruit orchards and executes a 90° turn to the south before reaching Tardebigge Old Wharf. The wharf, now a boatyard with moorings, was the temporary southern terminus of the canal from 1807 to 1815 and is located a short distance from the

Right The southern portal of Tardebigge Tunnel. Emerging from the tunnel the boat user is faced with descending 217ft through the Tardebigge flight of 30 locks. Nearby is the site of the founding of the Inland Waterways Association in 1946.

northern portal of the 580yd Tardebigge Tunnel. Emerging from the tunnel the boat user is faced with the daunting task of descending 217ft through the famous Tardebigge flight of 30 locks. Close to the top lock are moorings, a British Waterways maintenance yard and a plaque commemorating the founding of the Inland Waterways Association.

The Inland Waterways Association was formed in 1946 after the famous meeting at Tardebigge between Tom Rolt and Robert Aickman on the canal boat *Cressy*. This was a period when many of Britain's canal and river navigations were abandoned or derelict and in danger of being lost forever. The Association's founder members believed that waterways were part of our heritage and saw a way of life that was part of our history disappearing. They also saw vast recreational potential and the hope of revitalising inland water transport. The IWA is proud to look back and to celebrate the achievements of over fifty years' work for waterways. Today the campaign continues, for the improvement of

Left The former canal engine house at Lock 57, now a restaurant and bar, once maintained water levels to the summit of the Tardebigge flight of locks by back-pumping water from nearby Tardebigge Reservoir.

the existing waterways network, the retention of navigations still under threat and the preservation of the historical environment and for the extension of the system by reopening derelict waterways and creating new links. (Inland Waterways Association, 114 Regent's Park Road, London NW1 8UQ. Tel. 0171 586 2556/2510)

Tardebigge top lock is the site of a vertical boat lift, temporarily installed by the engineer John Woodhouse in 1811. Although successful during tests, the canal company decided to replace it by a conventional lock, at 14ft one of the deepest on the canal system. Located close to the next lock in the flight is the former canal engine house, now a restaurant and bar, that once maintained water levels to the summit by

Right A narrowboat enters Lock 41 at the appropriately named Half-Way House Bridge. Teamwork is vital for speeding up journey times through the Tardebigge flight of locks.

Right Working up the Tardebigge flight of locks is a slow business with plenty of time to enjoy the rural delights of the Worcestershire countryside.

back-pumping water from Tardebigge Reservoir. A journey down the flight, one of the wonders of the canal world, either by boat or on foot, is a rewarding experience. The canal wends its way down through the Worcestershire hills, each lock making a pretty sight with its traditional black and white painted paddles and wooden gates. Small cottages with well-tended gardens are tucked in at intervals along the rural route and the popular Queen's Head canalside pub is conveniently located at the foot of the flight, between locks 28 and 29. One mile to the north-west of the pub is Avoncroft Museum of Buildings, featuring restored buildings dating from the 14th-18th centuries.

From the bottom lock of the flight a further six locks take the canal down to the small village of Stoke Prior and Stoke Wharf where there is a boatyard, moorings and the popular canalside Navigation public house. To the west the Birmingham to Gloucester railway line hoves

Right Louise passes under Half-Way House Bridge to enter a lock on the Tardebigge flight, one of the wonders of the canal world.

into view as it parallels the canal's route for the next six miles to Tibberton. Half a mile south of Stoke Wharf the canal passes Stoke Works, the site of a major brine extraction industry responsible for much of the canal's trade in the 19th century. Since Roman times salt extraction had been an important industry in the area surrounding the nearby town of Droitwich. Towards the end of the 18th century large deposits of underground brine were discovered in the Stoke Prior area and these were developed into one of the largest salt works in the world. Opened in 1828, the works were eventually dispatching several hundred thousand tons of salt each year, initially all of it by boat on the Worcester & Birmingham Canal. Most of this traffic was lost when the newly-opened Birmingham & Gloucester Railway started to transport the salt in 1847. The salt company, owning its own canal boats and railway trucks, was eventually taken over by the mighty Imperial Chemical

Left *Lock 28 is the top of the Stoke flight of six locks. However, there is only a short respite and a canalside pub before the bottom lock of the Tardebigge flight is reached.*

Industries who eventually closed the works in 1970. The Butcher's Arms and the Boat & Railway are two popular canalside pubs located to the south of Stoke Works.

The six Astwood Locks, located to the south-west of Stoke Works and spread over a distance of one mile alongside the railway line, drop the canal down towards Hanbury Wharf, en route passing under the Birmingham to Gloucester railway line. Hanbury Wharf, junction with the former Droitwich Junction Canal, is the location for the popular Eagle & Sun canalside public house. The bridge over the canal carries the road originally built by the Romans to transport the salt that was extracted in Droitwich.

The Droitwich Junction Canal was opened in 1852 in a vain attempt by the Worcester & Birmingham canal to regain the salt traffic lost to the railways in 1847. The canal, 1¾ miles in length with seven locks, connected with the Droitwich Barge Canal which, in turn, joined with

Right The boatyard and moorings at Hanbury Wharf are conveniently located close to the Eagle & Sun canalside pub. A short arm of the former Droitwich Junction Canal, which meets the Worcester & Birmingham at Hanbury, is also used for moorings.

the River Severn at Hawford. After years of neglect it was officially abandoned in 1939 and is now the subject of a complete restoration scheme. The Droitwich Canals Trust was formed to restore both the Droitwich Barge and Junction Canals and welcomes volunteer working parties.

Temporarily parting company with the railway, the Worcester & Birmingham Canal continues on its southerly route through the Worcestershire countryside, rejoining it one mile south of Hanbury Wharf at Dunhampstead Tunnel. As with the others on the canal, the 236yd tunnel has no towpath and walkers must follow the former horse path through the woods. At the southern end of the tunnel are a boatyard, moorings and the popular canalside Fir Tree Inn. At nearby Oddingley, with its picturesque church and half-timbered farm, the railway parts company with the canal for the last time as the latter veers west towards the small village of Tibberton. Conveniently situated in

Left *A narrowboat prepares to enter Lock 15 on the Offerton flight of locks. A short distance beyond, the M5 motorway provides a stark contrast to this leisurely form of travel.*

the village for both boat users and walkers are a post office and the Speed the Plough and The Bridge canalside pubs. Departing from Tibberton the canal is soon crossed by the busy M5 motorway and immediately encounters the first of the six Offerton flight of locks which drop the canal a further 42ft down towards the River Severn. Soon, the industrial outskirts of the City of Worcester come into view as the canal passes through Tolladine and Blackpole locks. Between the latter lock and the railway bridge which crosses the canal to the west is the site of a wharf that once saw much canal-borne trade to and from Cadbury's factories at Bourneville and Frampton-on-Severn in Gloucestershire. Four more locks drop the Worcester & Birmingham Canal a further 28ft down into the city where it is now accompanied by a well-tended towpath much used by local residents. At Bridge 12, just beyond the lower of the four locks and close to the football ground is the Cavalier Tavern canalside pub.

The busy City of Worcester, once home to the composer Sir Edward Elgar, is rich in history, historic architecture and museums. Renowned for its world-famous Royal Worcester porcelain, the city boasts a superb riverside 11th century cathedral, the 15th century Commandery, 15th century former Franciscan priory and the early 18th century Guildhall. Entering the heart of Worcester the canal passes under an unusual red-brick railway viaduct, carrying the Worcester to Hereford railway line, to the junction with Lowesmoor Wharf and basin. Here there is ample mooring space and the canalside Bridge Inn. From Lowesmoor to Diglis Basin the canal is spanned by eight bridges and passes through the two final narrow locks at Blockhouse and Sidbury. Close to Sidbury Lock, or King's Head as it was once known, are the Red Lion and King's Head canalside inns. The Commandery, located close to the lock, is a 15th century timber building that became the headquarters of Royalist soldiers during the Civil War. In the ensuing Battle of Worcester in 1651 hundreds of the soldiers were killed in the bloody battle with Cromwell's army. The historic building with its fine Elizabethan interior is open to the public.

Nearing its junction with the River Severn the Worcester &

Birmingham Canal enters the two Diglis Basins. This large expanse of water was opened in 1815 and was once busy with the transshipment of goods between commercial canal and river craft. Complete with boat yards and a dry dock the basins, surrounded by former warehouses, now provide moorings for a large number of canal pleasure boats. Two wide locks, overlooked by the Royal Worcester porcelain factory, finally links the canal with the fast-flowing River Severn.

Left *Home sweet home amidst the clutter of Diglis Basin, Worcester.*

BIBLIOGRAPHY

Atterbury P., *Exploring Britain's Canals*, HarperCollins, 1994

Essex-Lopestri M., *Exploring the Regent's Canal*, Brewin Books, 1987

Gotch C., *The Gloucester & Sharpness Canal and Robert Mylne*, Lantern Press, 1993

Conway-Jones H., *A Guide to Gloucester Docks*, Alan Sutton, 1988

Ordnance Survey Guide to the Waterways 1: South, Nicholson/Ordnance Survey, 1983

Ordnance Survey Guide to the Waterways 2: Central, Nicholson/Ordnance Survey, 1983

Ordnance Survey Guide to the Waterways 3: North, Nicholson/Ordnance Survey, 1983

Hadfield C., *The Canals of the British Isles* (series of regional guides), David & Charles

Holland J. A., *Canal Recollections*, Parkgate Books, 1998

McKnight H., *The Shell Book of Inland Waterways*, David & Charles, 1975

Rolt L.T.C., *Narrow Boat*, Eyre & Spottiswoode, 1944

Poole J., *Narrow Boat Venture*, Thornhill Press, 1975

Quinlan R., *Canal Walks: Midlands*, Alan Sutton, 1992

Morris J., *Shropshire Union Canal*, Management Update, 1991

Pearson J.M., *Pearson's Canal & River Companion: Severn & Avon*, J.M.Pearson & Son, 1994

Pearson J.M., *Pearson's Canal & River Companion: Grand Union, Oxford*, J.M.Pearson & Son, 1994

Pearson J.M., *Pearson's Canal & River Companion: Shropshire Union & Llangollen Canals*, J.M.Pearson & Son, 1994